Building Microservices with .NET Core

Transitioning monolithic architecture using microservices with .NET Core

Gaurav Kumar Aroraa
Lalit Kale
Kanwar Manish

BIRMINGHAM - MUMBAI

Building Microservices with .NET Core

First published: June 2017

Production reference: 1120617

Published by Packt Publishing Ltd.
Livery Place
35 Livery Street
Birmingham
B3 2PB, UK.
ISBN 978-1-78588-783-3

www.packtpub.com

Credits

Authors
Gaurav Kumar Aroraa
Lalit Kale
Kanwar Manish

Reviewers
Vidya Vrat Agarwal
Nishith Shukla

Commissioning Editor
Veena Pagare

Acquisition Editor
Denim Pinto

Content Development Editor
Vikas Tiwari

Technical Editor
Diwakar Shukla

Copy Editor
Gladson Monteiro

Project Coordinator
Ulhas Kambali

Proofreader
Safis Editing

Indexer
Tejal Daruwale Soni

Graphics
Abhinash Sahu

Production Coordinator
Shantanu N. Zagade

Foreword

"Our industry does not respect tradition – it only respects innovation."
- Satya Nadella

I've spent my last three years at Microsoft, running customer feedback programs for Azure microservice architectures and tooling. I believe this microservices framework is a crucial spark of innovation in web development. In an agile world, we need an agile framework on the cloud that is working for us, processing individual actors and services. With this new power, we can deploy a framework that scales, improves resiliency, greatly reduces latency, increases our control of security, and upgrades the system without downtime. Microservices becomes the optimal architecture in our new cloud-based development environment, and it can result in major cost benefits.

Gaurav Aroraa, Lalit Kale, and Manish Kanwar masterfully whisk us away on a journey to explore the history of microservices, and they carefully and thoroughly take us on a tour of the architectural design concepts that accompany the evolution of microservices, from when James Lewis first coined the term to our current tools and implementations. The book starts at a high level, with detailed diagrams and descriptions that explain the architectural scenarios and uncovers all the values you'll receive with a microservices design. At this point, you might ask whether the book is about microservices architecture or a how-to guide in .NET development. Importantly, the authors transition us into the practical knowledge of translating our current applications into this bold new world of microservices. On that journey, they do not speed up. In other books, you move so fast that you simply cannot enjoy the view (or understand what you're supposed to be learning). You might just implement the code and pick up a few tactics along the way, mostly copying and coding by autopilot. But the authors teach each concept and step in the development process with the attention and focus that it deserves.

Personally, I have had the privilege of knowing Gaurav for a few years now. He's a Visual Studio and Development MVP (Microsoft's Most Valuable Professional award) and a key leader in the Microsoft cloud development community. I've worked closely with him on his powerful contributions on TechNet Wiki. In this book, I see a dedication and passion from Gaurav, Lalit, and Manish shine through. This book needs to be written. I am excited when I find gems like this. The authors thoroughly go through every detail, every parameter, and every consideration in tackling this weighty concept of a microservices architecture in .NET development. Read this book, skip ahead where you're knowledgeable about the given information, absorb the authors' knowledge, and share the book with your business contacts. The development community needs to adopt a microservices approach, and this book is a powerful advocate on that journey.

Ed Price

Senior Program Manager

Microsoft AzureCAT (Customer Advisory Team), Microservices and Cloud Development

Co-Author of *Learn to Program with Microsoft Small Basic*

About the Authors

Gaurav Kumar Aroraa has done M.Phil in computer science. He is a Microsoft MVP, certified as a scrum trainer/coach, XEN for ITIL-F, and APMG for PRINCE-F and PRINCE-P. Gaurav serves as a mentor at IndiaMentor, webmaster of dotnetspider, contributor to TechNet Wiki, and co-founder of Innatus Curo Software LLC. In the 19+ years of his career, he has mentored thousands of students and industry professionals. You can reach Gaurav via his blog, LinkedIn, and twitter handle (`@g_arora`).

Book writing is not an easy job, as it takes a lot of time. Sometimes, it needs your personal/family time. So, I want to thank all who motivated me and allowed me to spend time on this book, time that I was supposed to spend with them. My first thank you is to my wife, Shuby Arora, for her support in all ways. Then, I would like to thank my angel, Aarchi Arora (the newest member of our family). A great thanks to my parents whose blessings are always with me; this is because of them. I would like to thank the entire Packt team, especially Vikas Tiwari and Denim Pinto for their overnight support. A great thank you to Ed Price for his in-depth knowledge and his suggestions to improve various sections of the book. Finally, I want to say thanks to both Lalit and Manish for their full support as co-authors and their reply when I need for the book discussion.

Lalit Kale is a technical architect and consultant with more than 12 years of industry experience. Lalit has helped clients achieve tangible business outcomes through the implementation of best practices in software development. He is a practitioner of TDD and DDD, and a big believer in agile and lean methodologies. He has worked with several organizations, from start-ups to large enterprises, in making their systems successful, be it in-house or mission critical, with clients in the USA, the UK, Germany, Ireland, and India. His current interests include container technologies and machine learning using Python. He holds a bachelor's degree in engineering (IT).

I would like to take this opportunity to thank my coauthors, Gaurav and Manish, and the entire Packt team, without whom this book would never have existed. I would also like to thank Lord Ganesha and my parents. Without their support, I would never have been creative and wouldn't have pursued my passion with computers. I would like to pay my respect to my source of inspiration--my beloved grandfather, Raghunath Savdekar, who passed away during the writing of this book. Grandpa, this book is for you.

Lastly, I'd like to acknowledge the support from my wife, Sonal, and my kid, Aaryan, who had to tolerate my demands for endless cups of coffee and peaceful silence during long writing nights.

Kanwar Manish completed his masters of science in computer applications from MD University, India, and is a cofounder of Innatus Curo Software LLC, with a presence in India. He has been working in the IT industry across domains for the last 17 years. He started exploring .NET right from the first release and has been glued to it ever since. His range of experience includes global wealth management (financial service industry, USA), life insurance (insurance industry, USA), and document management system (DMS), ECMS, India. Manish does his bit for the community by helping young professionals through the IndiaMentor platform.

I would like to thank my wife, Komal, and my young boys, Aadi and Veda, who had to bear my absence while I was still around and for giving me that crucial support. And a big thanks to the rest of my family for always encouraging me. Gaurav played a vital role in giving his valuable input in guiding me. Also, I'd like to acknowledge the support from Packt's editors.

About the Reviewers

Vidya Vrat Agarwal is software technology enthusiast, Microsoft MVP, C# Corner MVP, TOGAF Certified Architect, Certified Scrum Master (CSM), and a published author. He has presented sessions at various technical conferences and code camps in India and the USA. He lives in Redmond, WA with his wife Rupali and two daughters, Pearly and Arshika. He is passionate about .NET and works as a software architect/.NET consultant. He can be followed on Twitter at @DotNetAuthor.

Nishith Shukla is a seasoned software architect and has been a leader in developing software products for over 15 years. Currently, he is working in Bay Area, California for BlackBerry. He joined BlackBerry through the acquisition of AtHoc and is playing a key technical leadership role in transmitting BlackBerry from a hardware to a software company.
Nishith has played a key role in various software products through his extensive knowledge on OOP, design patterns, and architectural best practices, including microservices, and through his balanced approach between business goals and technical goals. Outside work, Nishith plays an active role in software community building, playing Golf, travelling the world, and spending time with his family.

www.PacktPub.com

For support files and downloads related to your book, please visit www.PacktPub.com.

Did you know that Packt offers eBook versions of every book published, with PDF and ePub files available? You can upgrade to the eBook version at www.PacktPub.comand as a print book customer, you are entitled to a discount on the eBook copy. Get in touch with us at service@packtpub.com for more details.

At www.PacktPub.com, you can also read a collection of free technical articles, sign up for a range of free newsletters and receive exclusive discounts and offers on Packt books and eBooks.

https://www.packtpub.com/mapt

Get the most in-demand software skills with Mapt. Mapt gives you full access to all Packt books and video courses, as well as industry-leading tools to help you plan your personal development and advance your career.

Why subscribe?

- Fully searchable across every book published by Packt
- Copy and paste, print, and bookmark content
- On demand and accessible via a web browser

Customer Feedback

Thanks for purchasing this Packt book. At Packt, quality is at the heart of our editorial process. To help us improve, please leave us an honest review on this book's Amazon page at `https://www.amazon.com/dp/1785887831`. If you'd like to join our team of regular reviewers, you can e-mail us at `customerreviews@packtpub.com`. We award our regular reviewers with free eBooks and videos in exchange for their valuable feedback. Help us be relentless in improving our products!

Table of Contents

Preface

Distributed systems are always difficult to get complete success with. Lately, microservices have been getting considerable attention. With Netflix and Spotify, microservices implementations have some of the biggest success stories in the industry. Microservices is quickly gaining popularity and acceptance with enterprise architects. On the other hand, there is another camp that thinks microservices as nothing new or only as a rebranding of SOA.

In any case, microservices architecture has critical advantages, particularly with regard to empowering the nimble improvement and conveyance of complex venture applications.

However, there is no clear practical advice on how to implement microservices in the Microsoft ecosystem and especially with taking advantage of Azure and the .NET Core framework.

This book tries to fill that void. It explores the concepts, challenges, and strengths of planning, constructing, and operating microservices architectures built with .NET Core. This book discusses all cross-cutting concerns, along with the microservices design. It also highlights the more important aspects to consider while building and operating microservices through practical *how tos* and best practices for security, monitoring, and scalability.

What this book covers

Chapter 1, *What Are Microservices?*, makes you familiar with microservices architectural styles, history, and how it differs from its predecessors, monolithic architecture and service-oriented architecture (SOA).

Chapter 2, *Building Microservices*, gives you an idea of the different factors that can be used to identify and isolate microservices at a high level, what the characteristics of a good service are, and how to achieve the vertical isolation of microservices.

Chapter 3, *Integration Techniques*, introduces synchronous and asynchronous communication, style of collaborations, and the API gateway.

Chapter 4, *Testing Strategies*, explores how testing microservices is different from testing a normal .NET application. It gets you acquainted with the testing pyramid.

Chapter 5, *Deployment*, covers how to deploy microservices and the best practices for it. It also takes into account the isolation factor, which is the key success factor, along with setting up continuous integration and continuous delivery to deliver business changes at a rapid pace.

Chapter 6, *Security*, describes how to secure microservices with OAuth and, also, container security and best practices in general.

Chapter 7, *Monitoring*, explains that debugging and monitoring microservices is not a trivial problem but a quite challenging one. We have used the word, *challenging*, on purpose--there is no silver bullet for this. There is no single tool in the .NET ecosystem that is, by design, made for microservices; however, Azure monitoring and troubleshooting is the most promising one.

Chapter 8, *Scaling*, explains that scalability is one of the critical advantages of pursuing the microservices architectural style. In this chapter, we will see scalability by design, and by infrastructure as well, with respect to the microservices architecture.

Chapter 9, *Reactive Microservices*, gets you familiar with the concept of reactive microservices. You will learn how you can build reactive microservices with the use of reactive extensions. The chapter will help you focus on your main task and free you from the chores of communicating across services.

Chapter 10, *Creating a Complete Microservices Solution*, will walk you through all the concepts of microservices that you have learned so far. Also, we will develop an application from scratch while putting all our skills to use.

What you need for this book

All supporting code samples in this book are tested on .NET Core 1.1, using Visual Studio 2015 update 3 as IDE and SQL Server 2008R2 as database on the Windows platform.

Who this book is for

This book is for .NET Core developers who want to learn and understand microservices architecture and implement it in their .NET Core applications. It's ideal for developers who are completely new to microservices or just have a theoretical understanding of this architectural approach and want to gain a practical perspective in order to manage application complexity better.

Conventions

In this book, you will find a number of text styles that distinguish between different kinds of information. Here are some examples of these styles and an explanation of their meaning.

Code words in text, database table names, folder names, filenames, file extensions, pathnames, dummy URLs, user input, and Twitter handles are shown as follows: "Here we are trying to showcase how our `Order` module gets abstracted."

A block of code is set as follows:

```
namespace FlixOne.BookStore.ProductService.Models
{
  public class Category
  {
    public Guid Id { get; set; }
    public string Name { get; set; }
    public string Description { get; set; }
  }
}
```

Any command-line input or output is written as follows:

```
Install-Package System.IdentityModel.Tokens.Jwt
```

New terms and important words are shown in bold. Words that you see on the screen, for example, in menus or dialog boxes, appear in the text like this: "Clicking the **Next** button moves you to the next screen."

Warnings or important notes appear in a box like this.

Tips and tricks appear like this.

Reader feedback

Feedback from our readers is always welcome. Let us know what you think about this book-what you liked or disliked. Reader feedback is important for us as it helps us develop titles that you will really get the most out of.

To send us general feedback, simply e-mail feedback@packtpub.com, and mention the book's title in the subject of your message.

If there is a topic that you have expertise in and you are interested in either writing or contributing to a book, see our author guide at www.packtpub.com/authors.

Customer support

Now that you are the proud owner of a Packt book, we have a number of things to help you to get the most from your purchase.

Downloading the example code

You can download the example code files for this book from your account at http://www.packtpub.com. If you purchased this book elsewhere, you can visit http://www.packtpub.com/support and register to have the files e-mailed directly to you.

You can download the code files by following these steps:

1. Log in or register to our website using your e-mail address and password.
2. Hover the mouse pointer on the **SUPPORT** tab at the top.
3. Click on **Code Downloads & Errata**.
4. Enter the name of the book in the **Search** box.
5. Select the book for which you're looking to download the code files.
6. Choose from the drop-down menu where you purchased this book from.
7. Click on **Code Download**.

Once the file is downloaded, please make sure that you unzip or extract the folder using the latest version of:

- WinRAR / 7-Zip for Windows
- Zipeg / iZip / UnRarX for Mac
- 7-Zip / PeaZip for Linux

The code bundle for the book is also hosted on GitHub at https://github.com/PacktPublishing/Building-Microservices-with-DotNET-Core. We also have other code bundles from our rich catalog of books and videos available at https://github.com/PacktPublishing/. Check them out!

Errata

Although we have taken every care to ensure the accuracy of our content, mistakes do happen. If you find a mistake in one of our books-maybe a mistake in the text or the code-we would be grateful if you could report this to us. By doing so, you can save other readers from frustration and help us improve subsequent versions of this book. If you find any errata, please report them by visiting http://www.packtpub.com/submit-errata, selecting your book, clicking on the **Errata Submission Form** link, and entering the details of your errata. Once your errata are verified, your submission will be accepted and the errata will be uploaded to our website or added to any list of existing errata under the Errata section of that title.

To view the previously submitted errata, go to https://www.packtpub.com/books/content/support and enter the name of the book in the search field. The required information will appear under the **Errata** section.

Piracy

Piracy of copyrighted material on the Internet is an ongoing problem across all media. At Packt, we take the protection of our copyright and licenses very seriously. If you come across any illegal copies of our works in any form on the Internet, please provide us with the location address or website name immediately so that we can pursue a remedy.

Please contact us at copyright@packtpub.com with a link to the suspected pirated material.

We appreciate your help in protecting our authors and our ability to bring you valuable content.

Questions

If you have a problem with any aspect of this book, you can contact us at questions@packtpub.com, and we will do our best to address the problem.

1

What Are Microservices?

The focus of this chapter is to get you acquainted with microservices. We will start with a brief introduction. Then, we will define its predecessors: monolithic architecture and **service-oriented architecture** (**SOA**). After this, we will see how microservices fare against both SOA and the monolithic architecture. We will then compare the advantages and disadvantages of each one of these architectural styles. This will enable us to identify the right scenario for these styles. We will understand the problems that arise from having a layered monolithic architecture. We will discuss the solutions available to these problems in the monolithic world. At the end, we will be able to break down a monolithic application into a microservice architecture. We will cover the following topics in this chapter:

- Origin of microservices
- Discussing microservices
- Understanding the microservice architecture
- Advantages of microservices
- SOA versus microservices
- Understanding problems with the monolithic architectural style
- Challenges in standardizing the .NET stack

Origin of microservices

The term *microservices* was used for the first time in mid-2011 at a workshop of software architects. In March 2012, James Lewis presented some of his ideas about *microservices*. By the end of 2013, various groups from the IT industry started having discussions on *microservices*, and by 2014, it had become popular enough to be considered a serious contender for large enterprises.

There is no official introduction available for *microservices*. The understanding of the term is purely based on the use cases and discussions held in the past. We will discuss this in detail, but before that, let's check out the definition of microservices as per Wikipedia (`http s://en.wikipedia.org/wiki/Microservices`), which sums it up as:

> *Microservices is a specialization of and implementation approach for SOA used to build flexible, independently deployable software systems.*

In 2014, James Lewis and Martin Fowler came together and provided a few real-world examples and presented *microservices* (refer to `http://martinfowler.com/microservices /`) in their own words and further detailed it as follows:

> *The microservice architectural style is an approach to developing a single application as a suite of small services, each running in its own process and communicating with lightweight mechanisms, often an HTTP resource API. These services are built around business capabilities and independently deployable by fully automated deployment machinery. There is a bare minimum of centralized management of these services, which may be written in different programming languages and use different data storage technologies.*

It is very important that you see all the attributes James and Martin defined here. They defined it as an architectural style that developers could utilize to develop a single application with the business logic spread across a bunch of small services, each having their own persistent storage functionality. Also, note its attributes: it can be independently deployable, can run in its own process, is a lightweight communication mechanism, and can be written in different programming languages.

We want to emphasize this specific definition since it is the crux of the whole concept. And as we move along, it will come together by the time we finish this book.

Discussing microservices

Until now, we have gone through a few definitions of *microservices*; now, let's discuss *microservices* in detail.

In short, a microservice architecture removes most of the drawbacks of SOA architectures. It is more code-oriented (we will discuss this in detail in the coming sections) than SOA services.

Slicing your application into a number of services is neither SOA nor microservices. However, combining service design and best practices from the SOA world along with a few emerging practices, such as isolated deployment, semantic versioning, providing lightweight services, and service discovery in polyglot programming, is microservices. We implement microservices to satisfy business features and implement them with reduced time to market and greater flexibility.

Before we move on to understand the architecture, let's discuss the two important architectures that have led to its existence:

- The monolithic architecture style
- SOA

Most of us would be aware of the scenario where during the life cycle of an enterprise application development, a suitable architectural style is decided. Then, at various stages, the initial pattern is further improved and adapted with changes that cater to various challenges, such as deployment complexity, large code base, and scalability issues. This is exactly how the monolithic architecture style evolved into SOA, further leading up to microservices.

Monolithic architecture

The monolithic architectural style is a traditional architecture type and has been widely used in the industry. The term *monolithic* is not new and is borrowed from the Unix world. In Unix, most of the commands exist as a standalone program whose functionality is not dependent on any other program. As seen in the succeeding image, we can have different components in the application such as:

- **User interface**: This handles all of the user interaction while responding with HTML or JSON or any other preferred data interchange format (in the case of web services).

- **Business logic**: All the business rules applied to the input being received in the form of user input, events, and database exist here.
- **Database access**: This houses the complete functionality for accessing the database for the purpose of querying and persisting objects. A widely accepted rule is that it is utilized through business modules and never directly through user-facing components.

Software built using this architecture is self-contained. We can imagine a single .NET assembly that contains various components, as described in the following image:

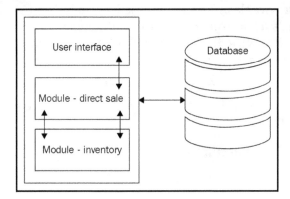

As the software is self-contained here, its components are interconnected and interdependent. Even a simple code change in one of the modules may break a major functionality in other modules. This would result in a scenario where we'd need to test the whole application. With the business depending critically on its enterprise application frameworks, this amount of time could prove to be very critical.

Having all the components tightly coupled poses another challenge: whenever we execute or compile such software, all the components should be available or the build will fail; refer to the preceding image that represents a monolithic architecture and is a self-contained or a single .NET assembly project. However, monolithic architectures might also have multiple assemblies. This means that even though a business layer (assembly, data access layer assembly, and so on) is separated, at run time, all of them will come together and run as one process.

A user interface depends on other components' direct sale and inventory in a manner similar to all other components that depend upon each other. In this scenario, we will not be able to execute this project in the absence of any one of these components. The process of upgrading any one of these components will be more complex as we may have to consider other components that require code changes too. This results in more development time than required for the actual change.

Deploying such an application will become another challenge. During deployment, we will have to make sure that each and every component is deployed properly; otherwise, we may end up facing a lot of issues in our production environments.

If we develop an application using the monolithic architecture style, as discussed previously, we might face the following challenges:

- **Large code base**: This is a scenario where the code lines outnumber the comments by a great margin. As components are interconnected, we will have to bear with a repetitive code base.
- **Too many business modules**: This is in regard to modules within the same system.
- **Code base complexity**: This results in a higher chance of code breaking due to the fix required in other modules or services.
- **Complex code deployment**: You may come across minor changes that would require whole system deployment.
- **One module failure affecting the whole system**: This is in regard to modules that depend on each other.
- **Scalability**: This is required for the entire system and not just the modules in it.
- **Intermodule dependency**: This is due to tight coupling.
- **Spiraling development time**: This is due to code complexity and interdependency.
- **Inability to easily adapt to a new technology**: In this case, the entire system would need to be upgraded.

As discussed earlier, if we want to reduce development time, ease of deployment, and improve maintainability of software for enterprise applications, we should avoid the traditional or monolithic architecture.

Service-oriented architecture

In the previous section, we discussed the monolithic architecture and its limitations. We also discussed why it does not fit into our enterprise application requirements. To overcome these issues, we should go with some modular approach where we can separate the components such that they should come out of the self-contained or single .NET assembly.

 The main difference between SOA & monolithic is not one or multiple assembly. But as the service in SOA runs as separate process, SOA scales better compared to monolithic.

Let's discuss the modular architecture, that is, SOA. This is a famous architectural style using which the enterprise applications are designed with a collection of services as its base. These services may be RESTful or ASMX Web services. To understand SOA in more detail, let's discuss *service* first.

What is service?

Service, in this case, is an essential concept of SOA. It can be a piece of code, program, or software that provides some functionality to other system components. This piece of code can interact directly with the database or indirectly through another service. Furthermore, it can be consumed by clients directly, where the client may either be a website, desktop app, mobile app, or any other device app. Refer to the following diagram:

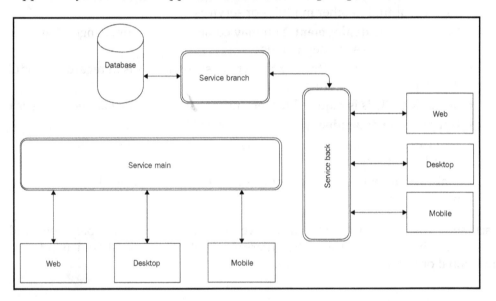

Service refers to a type of functionality exposed for consumption by other systems (generally referred to as clients/client applications). As mentioned earlier, it can be represented by a piece of code, program, or software. Such services are exposed over the HTTP transport protocol as a general practice. However, the HTTP protocol is not a limiting factor, and a protocol can be picked as deemed fit for the scenario.

In the following image, **Service – direct selling** is directly interacting with **Database**, and three different clients, namely **Web**, **Desktop**, and **Mobile**, are consuming the service. On the other hand, we have clients consuming **Service – partner selling**, which is interacting with **Service – channel partners** for database access.

A product selling service is a set of services that interacts with client applications and provides database access directly or through another service, in this case, **Service – Channel partner**. In the case of **Service – direct selling**, shown in the preceding example, it is providing some functionality to a Web Store, a desktop application, and a mobile application. This service is further interacting with the database for various tasks, namely fetching data, persisting data, and so on.

Normally, services interact with other systems via some communication channel, generally the HTTP protocol. These services may or may not be deployed on the same or single servers.

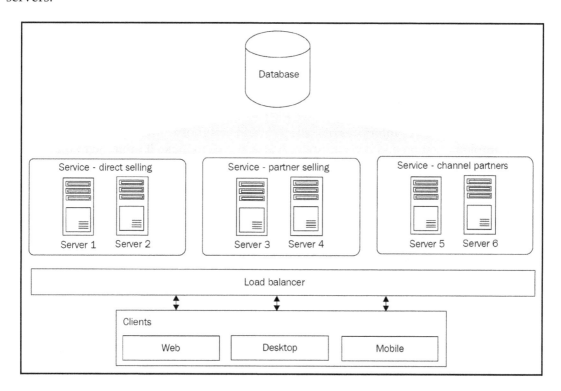

In the preceding image, we have projected an SOA example scenario. There are many fine points to note here, so let's get started. Firstly, our services can be spread across different physical machines. Here, **Service-direct selling** is hosted on two separate machines. It is a possible scenario that instead of the entire business functionality, only a part of it will reside on **Server 1** and the remaining on **Server 2**. Similarly, **Service – partner selling** appears to be having the same arrangement on **Server 3** and **Server 4**. However, it doesn't stop **Service – channel partners** being hosted as a complete set on both the servers: **Server 5** and **Server 6**.

A system that uses a service or multiple services in a fashion mentioned in the preceding figure is called an SOA. We will discuss SOA in detail in the following sections.

Let's recall the monolithic architecture. In this case, we did not use it because it restricts code reusability; it is a self-contained assembly, and all the components are interconnected and interdependent. For deployment, in this case, we will have to deploy our complete project after we select the SOA (refer to preceding image and subsequent discussion). Now, because of the use of this architectural style, we have the benefit of code reusability and easy deployment. Let's examine this in the wake of the preceding figure:

1. **Reusability**: Multiple clients can consume the service. The service can also be simultaneously consumed by other services. For example, *OrderService* is consumed by web and mobile clients. Now, *OrderService* can also be used by the Reporting Dashboard UI.
2. **Stateless**: Services do not persist any state between requests from the client, that is, the service doesn't know, nor care, that the subsequent request has come from the client that has/hasn't made the previous request.
3. **Contract-based**: Interfaces make it technology-agnostic on both sides of implementation and consumption. It also serves to make it immune to the code updates in the underlying functionality.
4. **Scalability**: A system can be scaled up; SOA can be individually clustered with appropriate load balancing.
5. **Upgradation**: It is very easy to roll out new functionalities or introduce new versions of the existing functionality. The system doesn't stop you from keeping multiple versions of the same business functionality.

Understanding the microservice architecture

The microservice architecture is a way to develop a single application containing a set of smaller services. These services are independent of each other and run in their own processes. An important advantage of these services is that they can be developed and deployed independently. In other words, we can say that microservices are a way to segregate our services so they can be handled completely independent of each other in the context of design, development, deployment, and upgrades.

In a monolithic application, we have a self-contained assembly of user interface, direct sale, and inventory. In the microservice architecture, the services part of the application changes to the following depiction:

Here, business components have been segregated into individual services. These independent services now are the smaller units that existed earlier within the self-contained assembly, in the monolithic architecture. Both **direct sales** and **inventory** services are independent of each other, with the dotted lines depicting their existence in the same ecosystem yet not bound within a single scope. Refer to the following diagram:

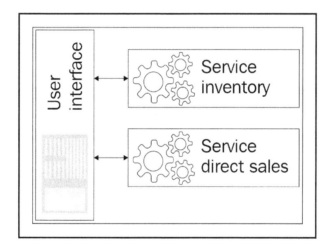

From the preceding image, it's clear that our user interface can interact with any of the services. There is no need to intervene in any service when a UI calls a service. Both the services are independent of each other, without being aware of when the other one would be called by the user interface. Both services are liable for their own operations and not for any other part in the whole system. Although much closer to the microservice architecture, the preceding visualization is not entirely a complete visualization of the intended microservice architecture.

 In the microservice architecture, services are small, independent units with their own persistent stores.

Now let's bring this final change so that each service will have its own database persisting the necessary data:

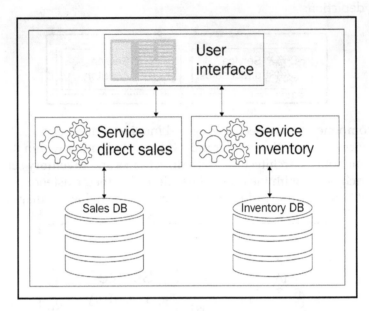

Here, **User interface** is interacting with those services that have their own independent storage. In this case, when a user interface calls a service for direct sales, the business flow for direct sales is executed independently of any data or logic contained within the inventory service.

The solution that the use of microservices provides has a lot of likely benefits, as discussed next:

- **Smaller codebase**: Each service is small, therefore, easier to develop and deploy as a unit
- **Ease of independent environment**: With the separation of services, all developers work independently, deploy independently, and no one is bothered about any module dependency

With the adoption of the microservice architecture, monolithic applications are now harnessing the associated benefits, as it can now be scaled easily and deployed using a service independently.

Messaging in microservices

It is very important to carefully consider the choice of the messaging mechanism when dealing with the microservice architecture. If this one aspect is ignored, then it can compromise the entire purpose of designing using the microservice architecture. In monolithic applications, this is not a concern as the business functionality of the components gets invoked through function calls. On the other hand, this happens via a loosely coupled web service level messaging feature, where services are primarily based on SOAP. In the case of the microservice messaging mechanism, it should be simple and lightweight.

There are no set rules for making a choice between various frameworks or protocols for a microservice architecture. However, there are a few points worth consideration here. Firstly, it should be simple enough to implement, without adding any complexity to your system. Secondly, it should be lightweight enough, keeping in mind the fact that the microservice architecture could heavily rely on interservice messaging. Let's move ahead and consider our choices for both synchronous and asynchronous messaging along with the different messaging formats.

Synchronous messaging

When a timely response is expected from a service by a system and the system waits on it till a response is received from the service, it is synchronous messaging. What's left is the most sought-after choice in the case of microservices. It is simple and supports HTTP request-response, thereby leaving little room to look for an alternative. This is also one of the reasons that most implementations of microservices use HTTP (API-based styles).

Asynchronous messaging

When a system is not immediately expecting a timely response from the service and the system can continue processing without blocking on that call, it is asynchronous messaging.

Let's incorporate this messaging concept into our application and see how it would change and look:

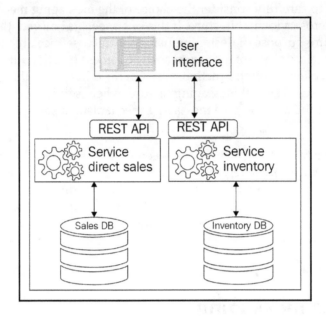

Message formats

Over the past many years, working with MVC and the like has got me hooked on the JSON format. You could also consider XML. Both the formats would do fine on HTTP with the API style resource. There are easily available binary message formats in case you need to use one. We are not recommending any format; you can go ahead with any of the selected message formats.

Why should we use microservices?

Tremendous patterns and architectures have been explored with some gaining popularity; there are others, though, which are losing the battle of Internet traffic. With each solution having its own advantages and disadvantages, it has become increasingly important for companies to quickly respond to fundamental demands, such as scalability, high performance, and easy deployment. Any single aspect failing to be not fulfilled in a cost-effective manner could easily impact large businesses negatively, making a likely difference between a profitable and non-profitable venture.

This is where we see *microservices* coming to the rescue of enterprise system architects. They can ensure their designs against problems quoted previously, with the help of this architectural style. It is also important to consider the fact that this objective is met in a cost-effective manner while respecting the factor of time involved.

How does the microservice architecture work?

Until now, we have discussed various things about the microservice architecture, and we can now depict how the microservice architecture works; we can use any combination as per our design approach or bet to a pattern that would fit in it. Here are a few points that favor the working of the microservice architecture:

- It's programming of the modern era, where we are expected to follow all SOLID principles. It's **object-oriented programming** (**OOP**).
- It is the best way is to expose the functionality to other or external components in a way so that any other programming language will be able to use the functionality without adhering to any specific user interfaces, that it, services (web services, APIs, rest services, and so on).
- The whole system works as per a type of collaboration that is not interconnected or interdependent.
- Every component is liable for its own responsibilities. In other words, components are responsible for only one functionality.
- It segregates code with a separation concept, and segregated code is reusable.

Advantages of microservices

Now let's try to quickly understand where microservices takes a leap ahead of the SOA and monolithic architectures:

- **Cost effective to scale**: You don't need to invest a lot to make the entire application scalable. In terms of a Shopping cart, we could simply load balance the product search module and the order-processing module while leaving out less frequently used operation services, such as inventory management, order cancellation, and delivery confirmation.

- **Clear code boundaries**: This action should match an organization's departmental hierarchies. With different departments sponsoring product development in large enterprises, this can be a huge advantage.

- **Easier code changes**: The code is done in a way that it is not dependent on the code of other modules and is only achieving isolated functionality. If it were done right, then the chances of a change in a microservice affecting another microservice are very minimal.

- **Easy deployment**: Since the entire application is more like a group of ecosystems that are isolated from each other, deployment could be done one microservice at a time, if required. Failure in any one of these would not bring the entire system down.

- **Technology adaptation**: You could port a single microservice or a whole bunch of them overnight to a different technology without your users even knowing about it. And yes, hopefully, you don't expect us to tell you that you need to maintain those service contracts, though.

- **Distributed system**: This comes implied, but a word of caution is necessary here. Make sure that your asynchronous calls are used well and synchronous ones are not really blocking the whole flow of information. Use data partitioning well. We will come to this little later, so don't worry for now.

- **Quick market response**: The world being competitive is a definite advantage, as otherwise, users tend to quickly lose interest if you are slow to respond to new feature requests or adoption of a new technology within your system.

SOA versus microservices

You'll get confused between microservices and SOA if you don't have a complete understanding of both. On the surface of it, microservices' features and advantages sound almost like a slender version of SOA, with many experts suggesting that there is, in fact, no need for an additional term, such as microservices, and that SOA can fulfill all the attributes laid out by microservices. However, this is not the case. There is enough difference to isolate them miles apart technologically.

The underlying communication system of SOA inherently suffers from the following problems:

- The communication system of SOA inherently suffers from the fact that a system developed in SOA depends upon its components, which are interacting with each other. So no matter how hard you try, it is eventually going to face a bottleneck in the message queue.
- Another focal point of SOA is imperative monogramming. With this, we lose the path to make a unit of code reusable with respect to OOP.

We all know how organizations spend more and more on infrastructure. The bigger the enterprise is, the more the complex is the question of ownership of the application being developed. With an increasing number of stakeholders, it becomes impossible to accommodate all of their ever-changing business needs. This is where microservices clearly stands apart. Although cloud development is not in the current scope of our discussion, it won't harm us to say that the scalability, modularity, and adaptability of the microservice architecture can be easily extended further with the use of cloud platforms. Time for a change.

Prerequisites of the microservice architecture

It is important to understand the resulting ecosystem from the microservice architecture implementation. The impact of microservices is not just preoperational in nature. So profound will the changes in any organization opting for the microservice architecture be that if they are not well prepared to handle it, it won't be long before advantages turn into disadvantages.

After the adoption of the microservice architecture is agreed upon, it would be wise to have the following prerequisites in place:

- **Deployment and QA**: Requirements would become more demanding, with a quicker turnaround from development requirements. It would require you to deploy and test as quickly as possible. If it is just a small number of services, then it would not be a problem. However, if the number of services is going up, it could very quickly challenge the existing infrastructure and practices. For example, your QA and staging environment may no longer suffice to test the number of builds that would come back from the development team.

- **A collaboration platform for development and operations team**: As the application goes to the public domain, it won't be long before the age-old script of Dev versus QA is played out again. The difference this time would be that the business will be at stake. So, you need to be prepared to quickly respond in an automated manner to identify the root cause when required.
- **A monitoring framework**: With the increasing number of microservices, you would quickly need a way to monitor the functioning and health of the entire system for any possible bottlenecks or issues. Without any means of monitoring the status of the deployed microservices and the resultant business function, it would be impossible for any team to take a proactive deployment approach.

Understanding problems with the monolithic architecture style

In this section, we will discuss all the problems with the monolithic .NET-stack-based application. In a monolithic application, the core problem is this: scaling monolithic is difficult. The resultant application ends up having a very large code base and poses challenges in regard to maintainability, deployment, and modifications.

Challenges in standardizing a .NET stack

In monolithic application technology, stack dependency stops the introduction of the latest technologies from the outside world. The present stack poses challenges as a web service itself suffers from some challenges:

- **Security**: There is no way to identify the user via webservices (no clear consensus on a strong authentication scheme). Just imagine a banking application sending unencrypted data containing user credentials without encryption. All airports, cafes, and public places offering free Wi-Fi could easily become victims of increased identity theft and other cybercrimes.
- **Response time**: Though the web services themselves provide some flexibility in the overall architecture, it quickly diminishes due to the high processing time taken by the service itself. So, there is nothing wrong with the web service in this scenario. It is a fact that a monolithic application involves huge code; complex logic makes the response time of a web service high, and therefore, unacceptable.

- **Throughput rate**: This is on the higher side, and as a result, hampers subsequent operations. A checkout operation relying on a call to the inventory web service that has to search for a few million records is not a bad idea. However, when the same inventory service feeds the main product searching/browsing for the entire portal, it could result in a loss of business. One service call failure out of ten calls would mean a 10 percent lower conversion rate for the business.

- **Frequent downtime**: As the web services are part of the whole monolith ecosystem, they are bound to be down and unavailable each time there is an upgrade or an application failure. This means that the presence of any B2B dependency from the outside world on the application's web services would further complicate decision-making, thereby seeking downtime. This absolutely makes the smaller upgrades of the system look expensive; thus, it further increases the backlog of the pending system upgrades.

- **Technology adoption**: In order to adopt or upgrade a technology stack, it would require the whole application to be upgraded, tested, and deployed, since modules are interdependent and the entire code base of the project is affected. Consider the payment gateway module using a component that requires a compliance-related framework upgrade. The development team has no option but to upgrade the framework itself and carefully go through the entire code base to identify any code breaks preemptively. Of course, this would still not rule out a production crash, but this can easily make even the best of the architects and managers sweat and lose some sleep.

Availability is a percentage of time during which a service is operating.

Response time is the time a service responds.

Throughput is the rate of processing requests.

Fault tolerance

Monolithic applications have high module interdependency as they are tightly coupled. The different modules utilize functionality in such an intramodule manner that even a single module failure brings the system down due to the cascading effect, which is very similar to dominoes falling. We all know that a user not getting results for a product search would be far less severe than the entire system coming down to its knees.

Decoupling using web services has been traditionally attempted at the architecture level. For database-level strategies, ACID has been relied upon for a long time. Let's examine both these points further.

- **Web services**: In the current monolithic application, customer experience is degraded due to this very reason. Even as a customer tries to place an order, reasons such as high response time of web services or WCF or even a complete failure of the services itself results in a failure to place the order successfully. Not even a single failure is acceptable as the users tend to remember their last experience and assume a possible repeat. Not only is this loss of possible sales, but also loss of future business prospects. Web services' failures can cause a cascading failure in the systems that rely on them.

- **ACID**: ACID is the acronym for atomicity, consistency, isolation, and durability; it's an important concept in databases. It is in place, but whether it's a boon or bane is to be judged by the sum total of the combined performance. It takes care of failures at the database level, and there is no doubt that it does provide some insurance against the database errors that creep in. But at the same time, every ACID operation hampers/delays operations by other components/modules. The point at which it brings the system where it causes more harm than benefit needs to be judged very carefully.

Scaling

Factors such as availability of different means of communication, easy access to information, and open world markets are resulting in businesses growing rapidly and diversifying at the same time. With this rapid growth of business, there is an ever-increasing need to accommodate an increasing client base. Scaling is one of the biggest challenges that any business faces while trying to cater for an increased user base.

Scalability is nothing but the capability of a system/program to handle the growth of work better. In other words, scalability is the ability of a system/program to scale.

Before starting the next section, let's discuss and understand scaling in detail, as this will be an integral part of our exercise as we work on transitioning from monolithic to microservices.

Scalability of a system is its capability to handle an increasing/increased load of work. There are two main strategies or types of scalability in which we can scale our application.

Vertical scaling or scale up

In vertical scaling, we analyze our existing application to find out the parts of modules that cause the application to slow down due to higher execution time. Making the code more efficient could be one strategy so that less memory is consumed. This exercise of reducing memory consumption could be for a specific module or the whole application. On the other hand, due to obvious challenges involved in this strategy, instead of changing the application, we could add more resources to our existing IT infrastructure, such as upgrading the RAM or adding more disk drives and so on. Both these paths in vertical scaling have a limit for the extent to which they could be beneficial. After a specific point in time, the resulting benefit will plateau out. It is important here to keep in mind that this kind of scaling requires downtime.

Horizontal scaling or scale out

In horizontal scaling, we dig deep into modules that show a higher impact on the overall performance for factors such as high concurrency; so this will enable our application to serve our increased user base, which is now reaching the million mark. We also implement load balancing to process a greater amount of work. The option of adding more servers to the cluster does not require downtime, which is a definite advantage. It differs from case to case and it needs to be seen whether all the additional cost of power, licenses, and cooling is worthwhile and up to what point.

 Scaling will be covered in detail in `Chapter 8`, *Scaling*.

Deployment challenges

The current application also has deployment challenges. It is designed as a monolithic application, and any change in the order module would require the entire application to be deployed again. This is time-consuming and the whole cycle will have to be repeated with every change. This means this could be a frequent cycle. Scaling could only be a distant dream in such a scenario.

As discussed in scaling about current application having deployment challenges which requires us to deploy the entire assembly. The modules are interdependent, and it is a single assembly application of .NET. The deployment of the entire application in one go also makes it mandatory to test the entire functionality of our application. The impact of such an exercise would be huge:

- **High-risk deployment**: Deploying an entire solution or application in one go poses a high risk as all modules are going to be deployed even for a single change in one of the modules.
- **Higher testing time**: As we have to deploy the complete application, we will have to test the functionality of the entire application. We can't go live without testing. Due to higher interdependency, the change might cause a problem in some other module.
- **Unplanned downtime**: Complete production deployment needs code to be fully tested and hence we need to schedule our production deployment. This is a time-consuming task that results in high downtime. Although planned downtime, during this time, both business and customers will be affected due to the unavailability of the system; this could cause revenue loss to the business.
- **Production bugs**: A bug-free deployment would be the dream of any project manager. However, this is far from reality and every team dreads this very possibility. Monolithic applications are no different from this scenario and productions bugs' resolution is easier said than done. The situation can only become more complex with some previous bug getting unresolved.

Organizational alignment

In a monolithic application, having a large code base is not the only challenge that you'll face. Having a large team to handle such a code base is one more problem that will affect the growth of the business and application.

- **Same goal**: In a team, all the team members have the same goal, which is timely and bug-free delivery at the end of each day. However, having a large code base and current, the monolithic architectural style will not be a comfortable feeling for the team members. With team members being interdependent due to the interdependent code and associated deliverables, the same effect that is experienced in the code is present in the development team as well. Here everyone is just scrambling and struggling to get the job done. The question of helping each other out or trying something new does not arise. In short, the team is not a self-organizing team anyway.

Roy Osherove defined three stages of a team in his book, *Teamleader*:

Survival phase: No time to learn

Learning phase: Learning to solve your own problems

Self-organizing phase: Facilitate, experiment

- **A different perspective**: The development team takes too much time for deliverables due to reasons such as feature enhancement, bug fixes, or module interdependency stopping easy development. The QA team is dependent upon the development team and the dev team has its own problems. The QA team is stuck once developers start working on bugs, fixes, or feature enhancements. There is no separate environment or build available for QA to proceed with their testing. This delay hampers overall delivery, and customers or end users would not get the new features or fixes on time.

Modularity

In respect to our monolithic application, where we may have an Order module, a change in the module *Orders* affects the module *Stock* and so on. It is the absence of modularity that has resulted in such a condition.

This also means that we can't reuse the functionality of a module within another module. The code is not decomposed into structured pieces, which could be reused to save time and effort. There is no segregation within the code modules, and hence, no common code is available.

Business is growing and its customers are growing by leaps and bounds. New or existing customers from different regions have different preferences when it comes to the use of the application. Some like to visit the website, but others prefer to use mobile apps. The system is structured in a way that we can't share the components across a website and a mobile app. This makes introducing a mobile/device app for the business a challenging task. Business is affected, as in such scenarios, the company loses out on customers who prefer mobile apps.

The difficulty in replacing the component's application using some third-party libraries; external system, such as payment gateways; and an external order-tracking system. It is a tedious job to replace the old components in the currently styled monolithic architectural application. For example, if we consider upgrading the library of our module that is consuming an external order-tracking system, then the whole change would prove to be very difficult. Also, it would be an intricate task to replace our payment gateway with another one.

In any of the preceding scenarios, whenever we upgraded the components, we upgraded everything within the application, which called for a complete testing of the system and required a lot of downtime. Apart from this, the upgrade would possibly result in the form of production bugs, which would require you to repeat the whole cycle of development, testing, and deployment.

Big database

Our current application has a mammoth database containing a single schema with plenty of indexes. This structure poses a challenging job when it comes down to fine-tuning the performance:

- **Single schema**: All the entities in the database are clubbed under a single schema named *dbo*. This again hampers business due to the confusion with the single schema regarding various tables that belong to different modules; for example, Customer and Supplier tables belong to the same schema, that is, *dbo*.
- **Numerous stored procedures**: Currently, the database has a large number of stored procedures, which also contain a sizeable chunk of the business logic. Some of the calculations are being performed within the stored procedures. As a result, these stored procedures prove to be a baffling task to tend to when the time comes to optimize them or break them down into smaller units.

Whenever deployment is planned, the team will have to look closely at every database change. This again is a time-consuming exercise and many times would turn out to be even more complex than the build and deployment exercise itself.

Prerequisites for microservices

To understand better, let's take up an imaginary example of Flix One Inc. With this example as our base, let's discuss all the concepts in detail and see what it looks like to be ready for microservices.

FlixOne is an e-commerce player (selling books) that is spread all over India. They are growing at a very fast pace and diversifying their business at the same time. They have built their existing system on the .NET framework, and it is a traditional three-tier architecture. They have a massive database that is central to this system, and there are peripheral applications in their ecosystem. One such application is for their sales and logistics team, and it happens to be an Android app. These applications connect to their centralized data center and face performance issues. FlixOne has an in-house development team supported by external consultants. Refer to the following figure:

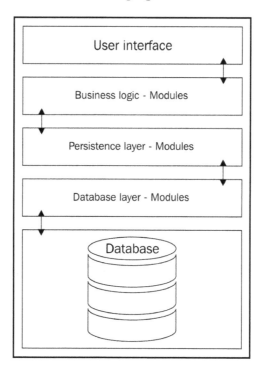

The preceding image depicts a broader sense of our current application, which is a single .NET assembly application. Here we have the user interfaces we use for search, order, products, tracking order, and checkout. Now check out the following diagram:

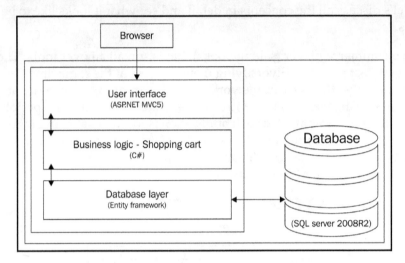

The preceding image depicts our **Shopping cart** module only. The application is built with C#, MVC5, and Entity Framework, and it has a single project application. This image is just a pictorial overview of the architecture of our application. This application is web-based and can be accessed from any browser. Initially, any request that uses the HTTP protocol will land on the user interface that is developed using MVC5 and JQuery. For cart activities, the UI interacts with the **Shopping cart** module, which is nothing but a business logic layer that further talks with the database layer (written in C#); data is persisted within the database (SQL Server 2008R2).

Functional overview of the application

Here we are going to understand the functional overview of the FlixOne bookstore application. This is only for the purpose of visualizing our application. The following is the simplified functional overview of the application until Shopping cart:

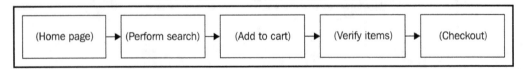

In the current application, the customer lands on the home page, where they see featured/highlighted books. They have the option to search for a book item if they do not get their favorite one. After getting the desired result, the customer can choose book items and add them to their shopping cart. Customers can verify the book items before the final checkout. As soon as the customer decides to check out, the existing cart system redirects them to an external payment gateway for the specified amount you need to pay for the book items in the shopping cart.

As discussed previously, our application is a monolithic application; it is structured to be developed and deployed as a single unit. This application has a large code base that is still growing. Small updates need to deploy the whole application at once.

Solutions for current challenges

Business is growing rapidly, so we decide to open our e-commerce website in 20 more cities; however, we are still facing challenges with the existing application and struggling to serve the existing user base properly. In this case, before we start the transition, we should make our monolithic application ready for its transition to microservices.

In the very first approach, the **Shopping cart** module will be segregated into smaller modules, then you'll be able to make these modules interact with each other as well as external or third-party software:

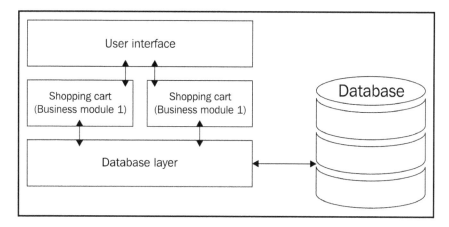

This proposed solution is not sufficient for our existing application, though developers would be able to divide the code and reuse it. However, the internal processing of the business logic will remain the same without any change in the way it would interact with the UI or the database. The new code will interact with the UI and the database layer with the database still remaining as the same old single database. With our database remaining undivided and as tightly coupled layers, the problems of having to update and deploy the whole code base will still remain. So this solution is not suitable for resolving our problem.

Handling deployment problems

In the preceding section, we discussed the deployment challenges we will face with the current .NET monolithic application. In this section, let's take a look at how we can overcome these challenges by making or adapting a few practices within the same .NET stack.

With our .NET monolithic application, our deployment is made up of xcopy deployments. After dividing our modules into different submodules, we can adapt to deployment strategies with the help of these. We can simply deploy our business logic layer or some common functionality. We can adapt to continuous integration and deployment. The xcopy deployment is a process where all the files are copied to the server, mostly used for web projects.

Making much better monolithic applications

We understand all the challenges with our existing monolithic application. We have to serve better with our new growth. As we are growing widely, we can't miss the opportunity to get new customers. If we miss fixing any challenge, then we would lose business opportunities as well. Let's discuss a few points to solve these problems.

Introducing dependency injections

Our modules are interdependent, so we are facing issues such as reusability of code and unresolved bugs due to changes in one module. These are deployment challenges. To tackle these issues, let's segregate our application in such a way that we will be able to divide modules into submodules. We can divide our `Order` module in such a way that it would implement the interface, and this can be initiated from the constructor. Here is a small code snippet that shows how we can apply this in our existing monolithic application.

Here is a code example that shows our `Order` class, where we use the constructor injection:

```
namespace FlixOne.BookStore.Common
{
    public class Order : IOrder
    {
        private readonly IOrderRepository _orderRepository;
        public Order(IOrderRepository orderRepository)
        {
            _orderRepository = orderRepository;
        }
        public OrderModel GetBy(Guid orderId)
        {
            return _orderRepository.Get(orderId);
        }
    }
}
```

 The inversion of control or IoC is nothing but a way in which objects do not create other objects on whom they rely to do their work.

In the preceding code snippet, we abstracted our `Order` module in such a way that it could use the `IOrder` interface. Afterward, our `Order` class implements the `IOrder` interface, and with the use of inversion of control, we create an object, as this is resolved automatically with the help of inversion of control.

Furthermore, the code snippets of `IOrderRepository` and `OrderRepository` are as follows:

```
namespace FlixOne.BookStore.Common
{
    public interface IOrderRepository
    {
        OrderModel Get(Guid orderId);
    }
}
namespace FlixOne.BookStore.Common
{
    public class OrderRepository : IOrderRepository
    {
        public OrderModel Get(Guid orderId)
        {
            //call data method here
            return new OrderModel
            {
```

```
                    OrderId = Guid.NewGuid(),
                    OrderDate = DateTime.Now,
                    OrderStatus = "In Transit"
            };
        }
    }
}
```

Here we are trying to showcase how our `Order` module gets abstracted. In the preceding code snippet, we return default values for our order just to demonstrate the solution to the actual problem.

Finally, our presentation layer (the MVC controller) will use the available methods, as shown in the following code snippet:

```
namespace FlixOne.BookStore.Controllers
{
    public class OrderController : Controller
    {
        private readonly IOrder _order;
        public OrderController(IOrder order)
        {
            _order = order;
        }
        // GET: Order
        public ActionResult Index()
        {
            return View();
        }
        // GET: Order/Details/5
        public ActionResult Details(string id)
        {
            var orderId = Guid.Parse(id);
            var orderModel = _order.GetBy(orderId);
            return View(orderModel);
        }
    }
}
```

The following is a class diagram that depicts how our interfaces and classes are associated with each other and how they expose their methods, properties, and so on:

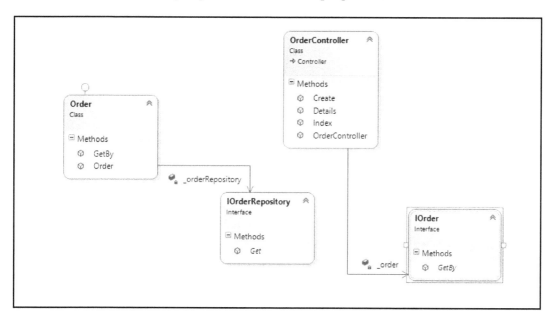

Here again, we used the constructor injection, where `IOrder` passed and got the `Order` class initialized; hence, all the methods are available within our controller.

By achieving this, we would overcome a few problems such as:

- **Reduced module dependency**: With the introduction of `IOrder` in our application, we are reducing the interdependency of the `Order` module. This way, if we are required to add or remove anything from/to this module, then other modules would not be affected, as `IOrder` is only implemented by the `Order` module. Let's say we want to make an enhancement to our `Order` module; it would not affect our `Stock` module. This way, we reduce module interdependency.
- **Introducing code reusability**: If you are required to get the order details of any of the application modules, you can easily do so using the `IOrder` type.
- **Improvements in code maintainability**: We have divided our modules into submodules or classes and interfaces now. We can now structure our code in such a manner that all the types, that is, all the interfaces, are placed under one folder and follow the suit for the repositories. With this structure, it would be easier for us to arrange and maintain code.

- Our current monolithic application does not have any kind of unit testing. With the introduction of interfaces, we can now easily perform unit testing and adopt the system of test-driven development with ease.

Database refactoring

As discussed in the preceding section, our application database is huge and depends on a single schema. This huge database should be considered while refactoring. We will go for this as:

- **Schema correction**: In general practice (not required), our schema depicts our modules. As discussed in previous sections, our huge database has a single schema, that is *dbo* now, and every part of the code or table should not be related to *dbo*. There might be several modules that will interact with specific tables. For example, our `Order` module should contain some related schema name, such as `Order`. So whenever we need to use the table, we can use them with their own schema instead of a general *dbo* schema. This will not impact any functionality related to how data would be retrieved from the database. But it will have structured or arranged our tables in such a way that we would be able to identify and correlate each and every table with their specific modules. This exercise will be very helpful while we are in the stage of transitioning of a monolithic application to microservices. Refer to the following image:

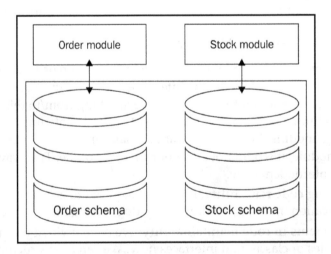

In the preceding figure, we see how the database schema is separated logically. It is not separated physically--our **Order Schema** and **Stock Schema** belong to the same database. So here we separate the database schema logically, not physically.

We can also take an example of our users: not all users are admin or belong to a specific zone, area, or region. But our user table should be structured in such a way that we should be able to identify the users by the table name or the way they are structured. Here we can structure our user table on the basis of regions. We should map our user table to a region table in such a way it should not impact or lay any changes in the existing codebase.

- **Moving business logic to code from stored procedures**: In the current database, we have thousands of lines **Stored Procedure** with a lot of business logic. We should move the business logic to our codebase. In our monolithic application, we are using Entity Framework; here we can avoid the creation of stored procedures. We can incorporate all of our business logic to code.

Database sharding and partitioning

Between database sharding and partitioning, we can go with database sharding, where we will break it into smaller databases. These smaller databases will be deployed on a separate server:

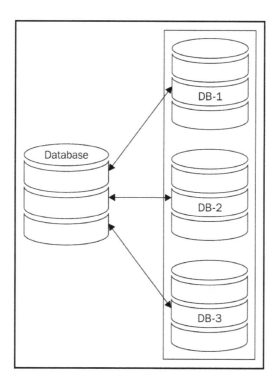

In general, database sharding is simply defined as a *shared-nothing* partitioning scheme for large databases. This way, we can achieve a new level of high performance and scalability. Sharding comes from *shard* and spreading, which means dividing a database into chunks(shards) and spreading to different servers.

The preceding diagram is a pictorial overview of how our database is divided into smaller databases.Take a look at the following diagram:

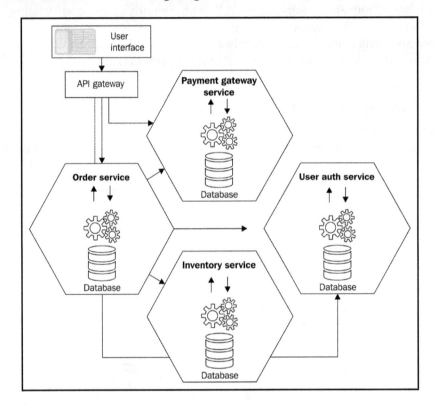

DevOps culture

In the preceding sections, we discussed the challenges and problems with the team. Here, we propose a solution to the DevOps team: the collaboration of the development team with another operational team should be emphasized. We should set up a system where development, QA, and the infrastructure team work in collaboration.

Automation

Infrastructure setup can be a very time-consuming job; developers would remain idle while the infrastructure is being readied for them. He or she will take some time before joining the team and contributing. The process of infrastructure setup should not stop a developer from becoming productive, as it would reduce overall productivity. This should be an automated process. With the use of Chef or PowerShell, we can easily create our virtual machines and quickly ramp up the developer count as and when required. This way, our developer can be ready to start the work from day one of joining the team.

Chef is a DevOps tool that provides a framework to automate and manage your infrastructure.

PowerShell can be used to create our Azure machines and to setup TFS.

Testing

We are going to introduce automated testing as a solution to our prior problems, those we faced while testing during deployment. In this part of the solution, we have to divide our testing approach as follows:

- Adopt **Test-Driven Development** (**TDD**). With TDD, a developer is required to test his or her own code. The test is nothing but another piece of code that could validate whether the functionality is working as intended. If any functionality is found to not satisfy the test code, the corresponding unit test fails. This functionality can be easily fixed, as you know this is where the problem is. In order to achieve this, we can utilize frameworks such as MS test or unit tests.
- The QA team can use scripts to automate their tasks. They can create scripts by utilizing QTP or the Selenium framework.

Versioning

The current system does not have any kind of versioning system. So there is no way to revert if something happens during a change. To resolve this issue, we need to introduce a version control mechanism. In our case, this should be either TFS or Git. With the use of version control, we can now revert to our change in case it is found to break some functionality or introduce any unexpected behavior in the application. We now have the capability of tracking the changes being done by the team members working on this application, at an individual level. However, in the case of our monolithic application, we did not have the capability of doing this.

Deployment

In our application, deployment is a huge challenge. To resolve this, we introduce **Continuous Integration (CI)**. In this process, we need to set up a CI server. With the introduction of CI, the entire process is automated. As soon as the code is checked in by any team member, using version control TFS or Git, in our case, the CI process kicks into action. It ensures that the new code is built and unit tests are run along with the integration test. In both the scenarios of a successful build or otherwise, the team is alerted to the outcome. This enables the team to quickly respond to the issue.

Next we move to continuous deployment. Here we introduce various environments, namely a development environment, staging environment, QA environment, and so on. Now as soon as the code is checked in by any team member, CI kicks into action. It invokes the unit/integration test suits, builds the system, and pushes it out to the various environments we have set up. This way, the turnaround time of the development team to provide a suitable build for QA is reduced to minimal.

Identifying decomposition candidates within monolithic

We have now clearly identified the various problems that the current Flix One application architecture and its resultant code is posing for the development team. Also, we understand which business challenges the development team is not able to take up and why.

It is not that the team is not capable enough--it is just the code. Let's move ahead and check what would be the best strategy to zero in on for the various parts of the Flix One application that we need to move to the microservice-styled architecture. You should know that you have a candidate with a monolith architecture, which poses problems in one of the following areas:

- **Focused deployment**: Although this comes at the final stage of the whole process, it demands more respect and rightly so. It is important to understand here that this factor shapes and defines the whole development strategy from the very initial stages of identification and design. Here's an example of this: the business is asking you to resolve two problems of equal importance. One of the issues might require you to perform testing for many more associated modules, and the resolution for the other might allow you to get away with limited testing. Having to make such a choice would be wrong. A business shouldn't have the option of making such a choice.

- **Code complexity**: Having smaller teams is the key here. You should be able to assign small development teams for a change that is associated with a single functionality. Small teams comprise one or two members. Any more than this and the need for a project manager should ring a bell in your ears. This means that something is more interdependent across modules than it should be.

- **Technology adoption**: You should be able to upgrade components to a newer version or a different technology without breaking stuff. If you have to think about the components that depend on it, you have more than one candidate. Even if you have to worry about the modules that this component depends upon, you still have more than one candidate. I remember one of my clients who had a dedicated team to test out whether the technology being released was a suitable candidate for their needs. I learned later that they would actually port one of the modules and measure the performance impact, effort requirement, and turnaround time of the whole system. I don't agree with this, though.

- **High resources**: Everything in a system from memory, CPU time, and I/O requirements should be considered a module in my opinion. If any one of the modules spends more time, and or more frequently, it should be singled out. In any operation that involves higher than normal memory, the processing time blocks the delay and I/O keeps the system waiting; this would be good in our case.

- **Human dependency**: If moving team members across modules seems like a herculean task that requires hand over, you have more candidates. Developers are smart, but if they have to struggle with large systems to get productive, it is not their fault. Break the system down into smaller units and you will have productive developers more easily.

Important microservices advantages

We have performed the first step of identifying our candidates for moving to microservices. It will be worthwhile going through the corresponding advantages that microservices provide.

Technology independence

With each one of the microservices being independent of each other, we now have the power to use different technologies for each microservice. The payment gateway could be using the latest .NET framework, whereas the product search could be shifted to any other programming language.

The entire application could be based on an SQL server for data storage, whereas the inventory could be based on NoSQL. The flexibility is limitless.

Interdependency removal

Since we try to achieve isolated functionality within each microservice, it is easy to add new features, fix bugs, or upgrade technology within each one. This will have no impact on other microservices. Now you have vertical code isolation that enables you to perform all of this and still be as fast with the deployments.

This doesn't end here. The Flix One team now has the ability to release a new option for the payment gateway alongside the existing one. Both the payment gateways could coexist till the time both the team and the business owners are satisfied with the reports. This is where the immense power of this architecture comes into play.

Alignment with business goals

It is not necessarily a forte of business owners to understand why a certain feature would be difficult or time-consuming to implement. Their responsibility is to keep driving the business and keep growing it. The development team should become a pivot to the business goal and not a roadblock.

It is extremely important to understand that the capability to quickly respond to business needs and adapt to marketing trends is not a by-product of microservices, but their goal.

The capability to achieve this with smaller teams only makes it more suitable to business owners.

Cost benefits

Each microservice becomes an investment for the business since it can easily be consumed by other microservices without having to redo the same code again and again. Every time a microservice is reused, time is saved by avoiding the testing and deployment of that part.

User experience is enhanced since the downtime is either eliminated or reduced to minimal.

Easy scalability

With vertical isolation in place and each microservice rendering a specific service to the whole system, it is easy to scale. Not only is the identification easier for the scaling candidates, but the cost is less. This is because we only scale a part of the whole microservice ecosystem.

This exercise can be cost-intensive for the business; hence, prioritization of which microservice should be scaled first can now be a choice of the business team. This decision no longer has to be a choice of the development team.

Security

Security is similar to what is provided by the traditional layered architecture; microservices can be secured as easily. Different configurations can be used to secure different microservices. You can have a part of the microservice ecosystem behind firewalls and another part to user encryption. Web-facing microservices could be secured differently from the rest of the microservices. You can suit your needs as per choice, technology, or budget.

Data management

It is common to have a single database in the majority of monolithic applications. And almost always, there is a database architect or a designated owner responsible for its integrity and maintenance. The path to any application enhancement that requires a change in the database has to go through this route. For me, it has never been an easy task. This further slows down the process of application enhancement, scalability, and technology adoption.

Because each microservice has its own *independent* database, the decision-making related to changes required in the database can be easily delegated to the respective team. We don't have to worry about the impact on the rest of the system, as there will not be any.

At the same time, this separation of the database brings forth the possibility for the team to become self-organized. They can now start experimenting.

For example, the team can now consider using the Azure Table storage or Azure Redis Cache to store the massive product catalog instead of the database, as is being done currently. Not only can the team now experiment, their experience could easily be replicated across the whole system as required by other teams in the form of a schedule convenient to them.

In fact, nothing is stopping the FlixOne team now from being innovative and using a multitude of technologies available at the same, then comparing performance in the real world and making a final decision. Once each microservice has its own DB, this is how Flix One will look:

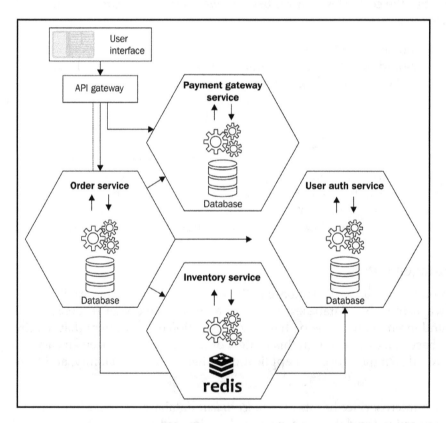

Integrating monolithic

Whenever a choice is made to move away from the monolithic architecture in favor of the microservice-styled architecture, the time and cost axis of the initiative would pose some resistance. Business evaluation might rule against moving some parts of the monolithic application that do not make a business case for the transition.

It would have been a different scenario if we were developing the application from the beginning. However, this is also the power of microservices in my opinion. A correct evaluation of the entire monolithic architecture can safely identify the monolithic parts to be ported later.

However, to ensure that these isolated parts do not cause a problem to other microservices in future, we must take one safeguard against the risk.

The goal for such parts of the monolithic application is to make them communicate in the same way as that of other microservices. Doing this involves various patterns and you utilize the technology stack in which the monolithic application was developed.

If you use the event-driven pattern, make sure that the monolithic application can publish and consume events, including a detailed modification of the source code to make these actions possible. This process can also be performed by creating an event proxy that publishes and consumes events. The event proxy can then translate these events to the monolithic application in order to keep the changes in the source code to a minimum. Ultimately, the database would remain the same.

If you plan to use the API gateway pattern, be sure that your gateway is able to communicate with the monolithic application. To achieve this, one option is to modify the source code of the application to expose RESTful services that can be consumed easily by the gateway. This can also be achieved by the creation of a separate microservice to expose the monolithic application procedures as REST services. The creation of a separate microservice avoids big changes in the source code. However, it demands the maintenance and deployment of a new component.

Summary

In this chapter, we discussed what the microservice architectural style is in detail, its history, and how it differs from its predecessors: monolithic and SOA. We further defined the various challenges that monolithic faces when dealing with large systems. Scalability and reusability are some definite advantages that SOA provides over monolithic. We also discussed the limitations of the monolithic architecture, including scaling problems, by implementing a real-life monolithic application. The microservice architecture style resolves all these issues by reducing code interdependency and isolating the dataset size that any one of the microservices works upon. We utilized dependency injection and database refactoring for this. We further explored automation, CI, and deployment. These easily allow the development team to let the business sponsor choose what industry trends to respond to first. This results in cost benefits, better business response, timely technology adoption, effective scaling, and removal of human dependency.

In the next chapter, we will go ahead and transition our existing application to the microservice-style architecture and put our knowledge to a real test.

2
Building Microservices

In the previous chapter, we discussed the problems of a layered monolith architecture. In this chapter, we will discuss how we can refactor them from the existing system and build separate microservices for product and order. In this chapter, we will cover the following topics:

- Size of microservices
- What makes a good service?
- Domain-driven design (DDD) and its importance for microservices
- The concept of Seam
- Communication between microservices
- Revisiting the case study--Flix One

Size of microservices

Before we start building our microservices, we should be clear about a few of its basic aspects, such as what factors to consider while sizing our microservices and how to ensure their isolation from the rest of the system.

As the name suggests, microservices should be micro. A question arises: what is micro? Microservices is all about size and granularity. To understand this better, let's consider the application discussed in `Chapter 1`, *What are Microservices?*

We wanted the teams working on this project to stay synchronized at all times with respect to their code. Staying synchronized is even more important when we make a release of the complete project. For this, we needed to first decompose our application/specific parts into smaller functionalities/segments of the main service. Let's discuss the factors that need to be considered for high-level isolation of microservices:

- **Risk due to requirement changes**: Changes in the requirements of one microservice should be independent of other microservices. In such a case, we will isolate/split our software into smaller services in such a way that if there are any requirement changes in one service, they will be independent of another microservice.
- **Functionality changes**: We will isolate the functionalities that are rarely changed from the dependent functionalities that can be frequently modified. For example, in our application, the customer module notification functionality will rarely change. But its related modules, such as Order, are more likely to have frequent business changes as part of their life cycle.
- **Team changes**: We should also consider isolating modules in such a way that one team can work independently of all the other teams. If the process of making a new developer productive--regarding the tasks in such modules--is not dependent on people outside the team, it means we are placed well.
- **Technology changes**: Technology use needs to be isolated vertically within each module. A module should not be dependent upon a technology or component from another module. We should strictly isolate the modules developed in different technologies or stacks or look at moving them to a common platform as our last resort.

We can say that our primary goal should not be to make services just as small as possible; instead, our goal should be to isolate the identified bounded context and keep it small.

What makes a good service?

Before microservices were conceptualized, whenever we thought of enterprise application integration, middleware looked like the most feasible option. Software vendors offered **Enterprise Service Bus (ESB)**, and it was one of the options as middleware.

Besides considering these solutions, our main priority should be inclined toward the architectural features. When microservices arrived, middleware was no more a consideration. Rather, the focus shifted to contemplation on business problems and how to tackle those problems with the help of the architecture.

In order to make a service that can be used and maintained easily by developers and users, it would require the service to have the following features (we can also consider these as characteristics of good services):

- **Standard data formats**: Good services should follow standardized data formats while exchanging with other components, services, or systems. The most popular data formats, also mostly used, in the .NET stack are XML and JSON.
- **Standard communication protocol**: Good services should obey standard communication formats, such as SOAP and REST.
- **Loose coupling**: One of the most important characteristics of a good service is that it follows loose coupling. When services are loosely coupled, we don't have to worry about changes. Changes in one service would not impact other services.

DDD and its importance for microservices

Domain-Driven Design (DDD) is a methodology and a process of designing complex systems. In this section, we will briefly discuss DDD and how it is important in the context of microservices.

Domain model design

The main objective of domain design is to understand the exact domain problems and then draft a model that can be written in any set of language/technologies. For example, in our Flix One bookstore application, we need to understand *Order Management* and *Stock Management*.

Here are a few characteristics of the domain-driven model:

- A domain model should focus on a specific business model and not across multiple business models
- It should be reusable
- It should be designed in a way that it should be called in the loosely coupled way, unlike the rest of the system

- It should be designed independently of persistence implementations.
- It should be pulled out from a project to another location, so it should not be based on any infrastructure framework.

Importance for microservices

DDD is the blueprint and can be implemented by microservices. In other words, once DDD is done, we can implement it using microservices. This is just like how in our application, we can easily implement *Order services, Inventory services, Tracking services*, and so on.

Once you have dealt with the transition process to your satisfaction, a simple exercise should be performed. This will help you verify that the size of the microservice is small enough. Every system is unique and has its own complexity level. Considering these levels of your domain, you need to have a baseline for the maximum number of domain objects that could talk to each other. If any service fails this evaluation criterion, then you have a possible candidate to evaluate your transition once again. However, don't get into this exercise with a specific number in mind; you can always go easy. As long as you have followed all the steps correctly, the system should be fine for you.

If you feel that this baseline process is difficult for you to achieve, you can take another route. Go through all the interfaces and classes in each microservice. Considering all the steps we have followed and the industry standard coding guidelines, anybody new to the system should be able to make sense of its purpose.

You can also perform another simple test to check whether the correct vertical isolation of the services was achieved. You can deploy each one of them and make them live with the rest of the services, which are still unavailable. If your service goes live and continues listening for incoming requests, you can pat your back now.

There are many benefits that you can derive from the isolated deployment capability. The capability to just deploy them independently allows the host in them to enter their own independent processes. It allows you to harness the power of the cloud and other hybrid models of hosting that you can think of. You are free to independently pick different technologies for each one of them as well.

The concept of Seam

At the very core of microservices lies the capability to work on a specific functionality in isolation from the rest of the system. This translates into all the advantages discussed earlier, such as reduced module dependency, code reusability, easier code maintenance, and better deployment.

In my opinion, the same attributes that were attained with the implementation of microservices should be maintained during the process of implementation. Why should the whole process of moving monoliths to microservices be painful and not be as rewarding as having the microservices itself? Just remember that the transition can't be done overnight and would need meticulous planning. Many capable solution architects have differed from my approach while presenting their highly capable teams. The answer lies not just in the points already mentioned but the risk to the business itself at the same time.

This is very well attainable. However, we must identify our way to the path correctly in order to achieve it. Otherwise, there is a possibility that the whole process of transitioning a monolithic application to microservices could be a dreadful one.

Module interdependency

This should always be the starting point when trying to transition a monolithic application to the microservice-styled architecture. Identify and pick up those parts of the application first that are least dependent on other modules and have the least dependency on them as well.

It is very important to understand that by identifying such parts of the application, you are not just trying to pick up the least challenging parts to deal with. However, at the same time, you have identified seams, which are the most easily visible ones. These are parts of the application where we will perform the necessary changes first. This would allow us to completely isolate this part of the code from the rest of the system. It should be ready to become a part of the microservice or deployed in the final stage of this exercise.

Even though such seams are identified, the capability to achieve the microservice-styled development is still a little farther away. This is a good start, though.

Technology

A two-pronged approach is required here. First, you must identify what different features of the application's base framework are being utilized. The differentiation could be, for example, on the basis of heavy dependency on certain data structures, interprocess communication being performed, or the activity of report generation. This is the easier part.

However, as the second step, I recommend that you become more confident and pick up pieces that use a type of technology that is different from what is being used currently. For example, there could be a piece of code relying upon simple data structures or XML-based persistence. Identify such baggage in the system and mark it for the transition. A lot of prudence is required in this twin-pronged approach. Making a pick that is too ambitious could embark us on a path similar to what we have been trying to avoid altogether.

Some of these parts might still not look like very promising candidates for the final microservice-styled architecture application. They should still be dealt with now itself. In the end, they would allow you to easily perform the transition.

Team structure

With every iteration of this identification process being executed, this factor becomes more and more important. There could be teams that are differentiated on various grounds, such as technical skill set, geographical location, or security requirements (employees versus outsourced).

If there is a part of the functionality that requires a specific skill set, then you could be looking at another probable Seam candidate. Teams can be composed of varying degrees of these differentiation factors. As part of the transition to microservices, the clear differentiation that could enable them to work independently could further optimize their productivity.

This can also provide a benefit in the form of safeguarding the intellectual property of the company--outsourcing to consultants for specific parts of the application is not uncommon. The capability to allow consultants or partners to help you only on a specific module makes the process simpler and secure.

Database

The heart and soul of any enterprise system is its database. It is the biggest asset of the system on any given day. It is also the most vulnerable part of the whole system in such an exercise. No wonder database architects can sound mean and intruding whenever you request them to make even the smallest of change. Their domain is defined by database tables and stored procedures.

The health of their domain is judged by the referential integrity and the time it takes to perform various transactions. I don't hold them guilty of overdoing it anymore. They have a reason for this; it is their past experiences. It's time to change that. Let me tell you this won't be easy, as we will have to utilize a completely different approach to handle data integrity once we embark on this path.

You might think that the easiest approach is to divide the whole database in one go, but this is not the case. It can lead us to the situation we have been trying to avoid all along. Let's see how to go about doing this in a more efficient manner.

As you move along, while picking up pieces after the module dependency analysis, identify the database structures that are being used to interact with the database. There are two steps that you need to perform here. First, check whether you can isolate the database structures in your code to be broken down and align it with the newly defined vertical boundaries. Second, identify what it would take to break down the underlying database structure as well.

Don't worry yet if you see that breaking down the underlying data structure is difficult. If it appears that it is involving other modules that you haven't started to move to microservices, it is a good sign. Don't let the database changes define the modules that you would pick and migrate to the microservice-styled architecture. Keep it the other way around. This ensures that when a database change is picked up, the code that depends on the change is already ready to absorb the change.

This ensures that you don't pick up the battle of data integrity while you are already occupied with modifying the code that would rely on this part of the database. Nevertheless, such database structures should draw your attention so that the modules that depend upon them are picked next. This will allow you to easily complete the move to microservices for all the associated modules in one go. Refer to the following diagram:

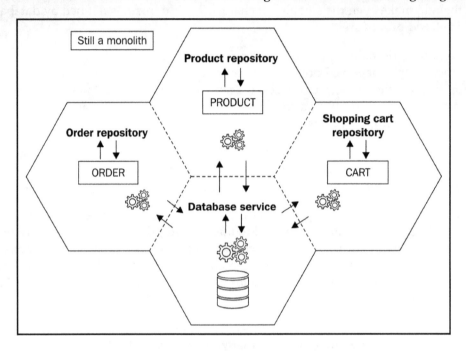

Here we have not broken the database yet. Instead, we have simply separated our database access part into layers as part of step one.

What we have simply done is that the code data structure mapped to the database no more has a dependency on each other. Let's see how this step would work out when we remove foreign key relationships.

However, if we can transition the code structures being used to access the database along with the database structure, we will save time. This approach might differ from system to system and can be affected by our personal bias. If your database structure changes seem to be impacting modules that are yet to be marked for transition, move on for now.

Another important point to understand here is what kind of changes are acceptable when you break down this database table or merge it with another partial structure? The most important one is not to shy away from breaking those foreign key relationships apart. This might sound like a big pushover from our traditional approach for maintaining data integrity. However, removing your foreign key relationships is the most fundamental challenge while restructuring your database to suit the microservice architecture. Remember that a microservice is meant to be independent of other services. If there are foreign key relationships with other parts of the system, it makes it dependent on the services owning that part of the database. Refer to the following diagram:

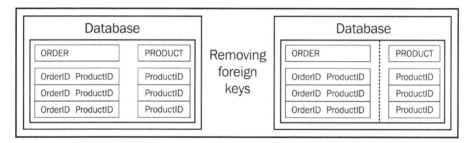

As part of step two, we have kept the foreign key fields in the database tables but have removed the foreign key constraint. So the **ORDER** table is still holding information about **ProductID** in the end, but the foreign key relation is broken now. Refer to the following diagram:

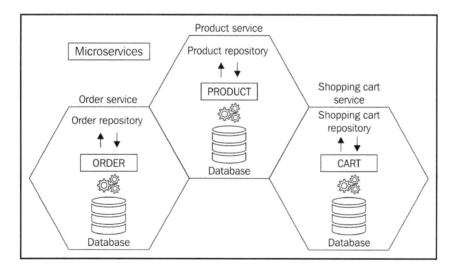

This is what our microservice-styled architecture would finally look like. The central database would be moved away in favor of each service having their own database. So, separating the data structures in the code and removing foreign key relationships is our preparation to finally make the change. The connected boundaries of microservices in the preceding figure signify the interservice communication.

With the two steps performed, your code is now ready to split **ORDER** and **PRODUCT** into separate services, with each having their own database.

If all of the discussion here has left you bewildered about all those transactions that have been safely performed upto now, you are not alone. This outcome of the challenge with the transactions is not a small one by any means and deserves focused attention. Let's talk about this in detail but a bit later. Before this, there is another part that becomes a no man's land in the database. It is master data or static data, as some may call it.

Master data

Handling master data is more about your personal choice and system-specific requirements. If you see that the master data is not going to change for ages and occupies an insignificant amount of records, you are better off with the configuration files or even code enumerations.

This requires someone to push out the configuration files once in a while when the changes do happen. However, this still leaves gap for future. As the rest of the system would depend on this one module, it will be responsible for these updates. If this module does not behave correctly, other parts of the system relying on it could also be impacted negatively.

Another option could be to wrap up master data in a separate service altogether. Having the master data delivered through a service would have the advantage of the services knowing the change instantly and understanding the capability to consume it as well.

The process of requesting this service might not be much different from the process of reading configuration files when required. It might be slower for once, but then it is to be done only as many times as necessary.

Moreover, you could also support different sets of master data itself. It would be fairly easy to maintain product sets that can differ every year. With the microservice-architecture style, it is always a good idea to be independent of any kind of outside reliance in future.

Transaction

With our foreign keys gone and the database split into smaller parts, we need to devise our own mechanisms for handling data integrity. Here, we need to factor in the possibility that not all services would successfully go through a transaction for the scope of their respective data stores.

A good example could be a user ordering a specific product. At the time the order is being accepted, there is sufficient quantity available to be ordered. However, by the time the order is logged, the Product service could not log the orders for some reason. We don't know yet whether this was due to insufficient quantity or some other communication fault within the system. There are two possible options here. Let's discuss them one by one.

The first option is to try again and perform the remaining part of the transaction sometime later. This would require us to orchestrate the whole transaction in a way that tracks individual transactions across services. So every transaction that leads to transactions being performed for more than one service must be tracked. In case one of them does not go through, it deserves a retry. This might work for long-lived operations.

However, for other operations, this could cast a real problem. If the operation is not long-lived and you still decide to retry, the outcome will result in either locking out other transactions or making the transaction wait--impossible to be completed.

Another option that we can contemplate here is to cancel the entire set of transactions spread across various services. This means that a single failure at any stage of the entire set of transaction would result in the reversal of all the previous transactions.

This will be one area where maximum prudence would be required, and it would be time well invested. A stable outcome is only guaranteed when the transactions are planned out well in any microservice-style architecture application.

Communication between microservices

In the preceding section, we separated our *Order module* into **Order Services** and discussed how we can break down the foreign key relationship between ORDER and PRODUCT tables.

In a monolithic application, we have a single repository that queries the database to fetch the records from both **ORDER** and **PRODUCT** tables. However, in our upcoming microservice application, we will segregate repositories between **Order Service** and **Product Service**. With each service having its respective database, each one would access its own database only. **Order Service** would only be able to access order **Database**, whereas **Product Service** would be able to access product **Database** only. **Order Service** should not be allowed to access product **Database** and vice versa. Refer to the following image:

 We will discuss communication between microservices in Chapter 3, *Integration Techniques*, in detail.

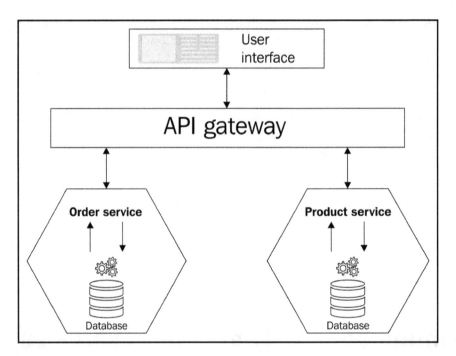

In the preceding figure, we see that our UI is interacting with **Order Service** and **Product service** via **API gateway**. Both the services are physically separated from each other and there is no direct interaction between these services. Communication performed in this manner is also referred to as communication that is based on the *API Gateway Pattern*.

The API gateway is nothing but a middle tier via which the UI can interact with the microservices. It also provides a simpler interface and makes the process of consuming these services simpler. It provides a different level of granularity to different clients as required (that is browser and desktop).

We can say that it provides coarse-grained APIs to mobile clients and fine-grained APIs to desktop clients, and it can use a high-performance network underneath its hood to provide some serious throughput.

The definition of granularity from `wiki`:

> **Granularity** *is the extent to which a system is broken down into small parts, either the system itself or its description or observation. It is the extent to which a larger entity is subdivided. For example, a yard broken into inches has finer granularity than a yard broken into feet.*
> *Coarse-grained systems consist of fewer, larger components than fine-grained systems; a coarse-grained description of a system regards large subcomponents while a fine-grained description regards smaller components of which the larger ones are composed.*

Benefits of the API gateway for microservices

There is no doubt that the API gateway is beneficial for microservices. With its use, you can do this:

- Services are invoked through the API gateway
- Round trips between the client and the application are reduced
- The client has the ability to access different APIs in one place, as segregated by the gateway

It provides flexibility to clients in such a manner that they are able to interact with different services as and when they need. This way, there is no need to expose complete/all services at all. API gateway is a component of complete API management. In our solution, we will use Azure API management and explain it further in `Chapter 3`, *Integration Techniques*.

API gateway versus API management

In the preceding section, we discussed how the API gateway hides the actual APIs from its client and then simply redirects the calls to the actual API from these clients. The API management solution provides a complete management system to manage all the APIs of its external consumers. Mostly, all API management solutions (such as Azure API management) provide various capabilities and functionalities, such as:

- Design
- Development
- Security
- Publishing
- Scalability
- Monitoring
- Analysis
- Monetization

Revisiting the case study--Flix One

In the preceding chapter, we took an example of an imaginary company, Flix One Inc., operating in the e-commerce domain and having its own .NET monolithic application: Flix One book store. We have already discussed:

- How to segregate the code
- How to segregate the database
- How to denormalize the database
- How to begin transitioning
- The available refactoring approaches

In this section, we will start writing/transitioning .NET monolith to a microservice application.

Prerequisites

We will use the following tools and technologies while transitioning our monolithic application to the microservice-styled architecture:

- Visual Studio 2015 or later
- C# 6.0
- ASP.NET Core MVC/Web API
- Entity Framework
- SQL Server

Transitioning to our product service

We already have our product module in place. We are going to pull back this module now and start with a new ASP.NET Core MVC project. For this, follow all the steps we discussed in the preceding sections and in Chapter 1, *What Are Microservices*? Let's see what technology and database we will use.

- **Technology stack**: We have already selected this for our product service; we will go with ASP.NET Core, C#, **Entity framework** (**EF**), and so on. Microservices can be written using different technology stacks and can be consumed by clients created in different technologies. For our product service, we will go with ASP.NET Core.
- **Database**: We have already discussed this in chapter 2, *Building Microservices*, when talking about a monolithic application and segregating its database. Here we will go with SQL Server, and the database schema would be Product instead of dbo.

Our product database is segregated. We will use this database in our product service, as shown in the following image:

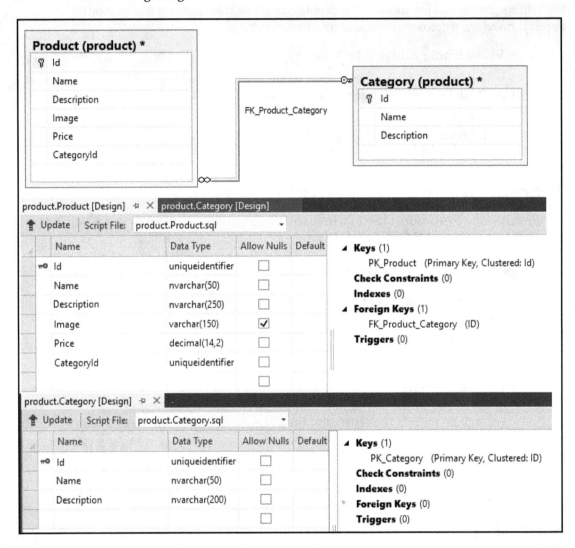

We have created a separated product database for our product service. We did not migrate the entire data. In the following sections, we will discuss product database migrations as well. Migration is important as we have numerous existing records of FlixOne book store customers. We can't ignore these records, and they need to be migrated to our modified structure. Let's get started.

Migrations

In the preceding section, we separated our product database to ensure that it would only be used by our product service. We also selected a technology stack of our choice to build our microservice (product service). In this section, we will discuss how we can migrate both our existing code and database to ensure that they fit right in with our new architectural style.

Code migration

Code migration does not involve just pulling out a few layers of code from the existing monolithic application and then bundling it with our newly created **Product service**. In order to achieve this, you'll need to implement all that you have learned until now. In the existing monolithic application, we have a single repository, which is common across all modules. Whereas, for microservices, we will create repositories for each module separately and keep them isolated from each other as well.

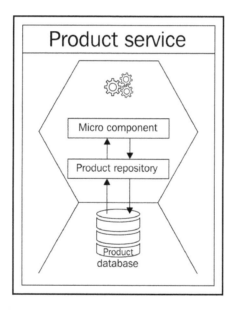

In the preceding image, **Product Service** has a **Product repository**, which further interacts with its designated data store, named **Product Database**. We can now discuss a bit about microcomponents as well. They are nothing but isolated parts within the application (microservice), namely common classes and business functionality. It is worthwhile to note here that the **Product repository** itself is a microcomponent in the world of microservices.

In our final product service, which is to be done in ASP.NET Core MVC, we will work with a model and controller to create our REST API. Let's talk about both of these briefly:

- **Model:** This is an object that represents the data in the product service. In our case, the identified models are stacked into product and category fields. In our code, models are nothing but a set of simple C# class. When we talk in terms of EF, they are commonly referred to as **plain old CLR objects** (**POCOs**). POCOs are nothing but simple entities without any data access functionality.
- **Controller:** This is a simple C# class that inherits an abstract class controller of the namespace `Microsoft.AspNetCore.Mvc`. It handles HTTP requests and is responsible for the creation of the HTTP response to be sent back. In our **Product Service**, we have a product controller that handles everything.

Let's follow a step-by-step approach to create our product service.

Creating our project

As already decided in the previous sections, we will create our ProductService in ASP.NET Core or C#, using Visual Studio. Let's see what steps are required to do this:

1. Start Visual Studio.
2. Create a new project by navigating to **File | New | Project.**
3. From the template options available, select **ASP.NET Core Web Application**, name it `FlixOne.BookStore.ProductService`, and click on **ok**.
4. Next, select **Web API** from the template screen and click on **ok**.

The following image depicts how our new solution should look:

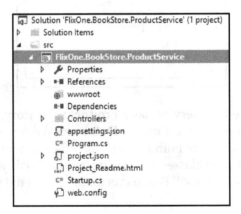

Adding the model

In our monolithic application, we do not have any model classes yet. So let's go ahead and add a new model as required. To add the new model, follow these simple steps:

- First, add a new folder and name it `Models`. In **Solution Explorer**, right-click on **project** and then click on **chose options** from **Add | New Folder:**

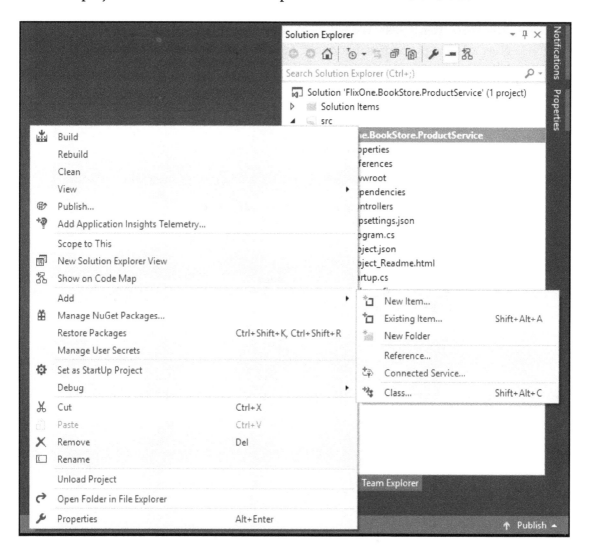

There is no hard and fast rule about putting all the model classes in a folder named `Models`. As a matter of fact, we can put our model classes anywhere in the project in our application. We follow this practice as it becomes self-explanatory from folder names. At the same time, it easily identifies that this folder is for the model classes.

To add new classes (these classes will represent our POCOs) Product and Category:

1. Right-click on the `Models` folder and chose **Option**.
2. Add **New Item|Class**. We will name them `Product` and `Category`.
3. Now add the properties that depict our product database column name from the tables `Product` and `Category`.

 There is no restriction for having the property name match the table column name. It is just general practice.

The following code snippet depicts what our `Product.cs` model class will look like:

```
namespace FlixOne.BookStore.ProductService.Models
{
    public class Product
    {
        public Guid Id { get; set; }
        public string Name { get; set; }
        public string Description { get; set; }
        public string Image { get; set; }
        public decimal Price { get; set; }
        public Guid CategoryId { get; set; }
    }
}
```

The following code snippet shows what our `Category.cs` model class will look like:

```
namespace FlixOne.BookStore.ProductService.Models
{
  public class Category
  {
    public Guid Id { get; set; }
    public string Name { get; set; }
    public string Description { get; set; }
  }
}
```

Adding a repository

In our monolithic application, we have a common repository throughout the project. In `ProductService`, by virtue of following all the principals learned until now, we will create microcomponents, which means separate repositories encapsulating the data layer.

A repository is nothing but a simple C# class that contains logic to retrieve data from the database and map it to the model.

Create a new folder and name it `Persistence`. Add the `IProduct` interface and a `Product` class that will implement the `IProduct` interface. Again, we named the folder `Persistence` in our effort to follow the general principal for easy identification. The following code snippet provides an overview of the `Product` class (it is still without any implementation and it does not have any interaction with the database yet):

```
namespace FlixOne.BookStore.ProductService.Persistence
{
    interface IProductRepository
    {
        void Add(Product Product);
        IEnumerable<Product> GetAll();
        Product GetBy(Guid id);
        bool Remove(Guid id);
        void Update(Product Product);
    }
}

namespace FlixOne.BookStore.ProductService.Persistence
{
    public class ProductRepository : IProductRepository
    {
        public void Add(Product Product)
        {
            throw new NotImplementedException();
        }
        public IEnumerable<Product> GetAll()
        {
            throw new NotImplementedException();
        }
        public Product GetBy(Guid id)
        {
            throw new NotImplementedException();
        }
        public bool Remove(Guid id)
        {
            throw new NotImplementedException();
        }
```

```
        public void Update(Product Product)
        {
            throw new NotImplementedException();
        }
    }
}
```

Registering the repositories

For `ProductService`, we will use built-in dependency injection support with ASP.NET Core. To do so, follow these simple steps:

1. Open `Startup.cs`.
2. Add the repository in the `ConfigureServices` method. It should look like this:

```
public void ConfigureServices(IServiceCollection services)
{
    // Add framework services.
    services.AddMvc();
    services.AddSingleton<IProductRepository, ProductRepository>();
}
```

Adding a product controller

Finally, we have reached the stage where we can proceed to add our controller class. This controller would be actually responsible for responding to the incoming HTTP requests with the applicable HTTP response. You can now get rid of the `ValueController` class, as it is a default class provided by the ASP.NET core template, in case you are wondering what is to be done with that.

Right-click on the `controllers` folder, chose the **Add ->New Item** option, and select **Web API Controller Class**. Name it `ProductController`. Here we are going to utilize whatever code/functionality we can from the monolithic application. Go back to the legacy code and see the operations you're performing there; they can be borrowed for our `ProductController` class. Refer to the following screenshot:

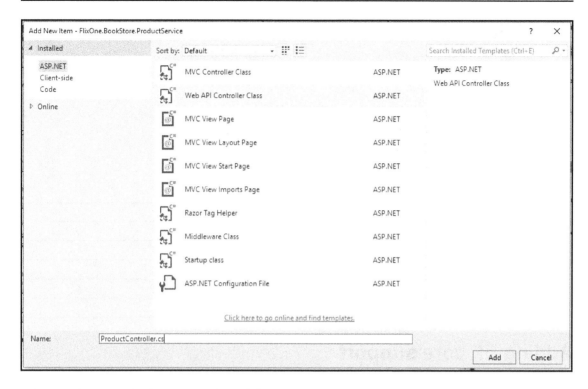

After we have made the required modifications to `ProductController`, it should look something similar to this:

```
using Microsoft.AspNetCore.Mvc;
using FlixOne.BookStore.ProductService.Persistence;
namespace FlixOne.BookStore.ProductService.Controllers
{
    [Route("api/[controller]")]
    public class ProductController : Controller
    {
        private readonly IProductRepository _ProductRepository;
        public ProductController(IProductRepository ProductRepository)
        {
            _ProductRepository = ProductRepository;
        }
    }
}
```

The ProductService API

In our monolithic application, for the `Product` module, we were doing the following:

- Adding a new `Product` module
- Updating an existing `Product` module
- Deleting an existing `Product` module
- Retrieving a `Product` module

Now we will create `ProductService`; we require the following APIs:

API Resource	Description
GET /api/Product	Get a list of products
GET /api/Product{id}	Get a product
PUT /api/Product{id}	Update an existing product
DELETE /api/Product{id}	Delete an existing product
POST /api/Product	Add a new product

Adding EF core support

Before going further, we need to add EF so that our service can interact with the actual product database. Until now, we did not add any method to our repository that could interact with the database.

To add EF core support, we need to add EF's core `sqlserver` package (we are adding the `sqlserrver` package because we are using SQL Server as our DB server). Open the `project.json` file and add the following package under dependencies:

```
"Microsoft.EntityFrameworkCore.SqlServer": "1.1.0"
```

Otherwise, the same package can be added using NuGet Package Manager. Just open NuGet package and search for `Microsoft.EntityFrameworkCore.SqlServer`:

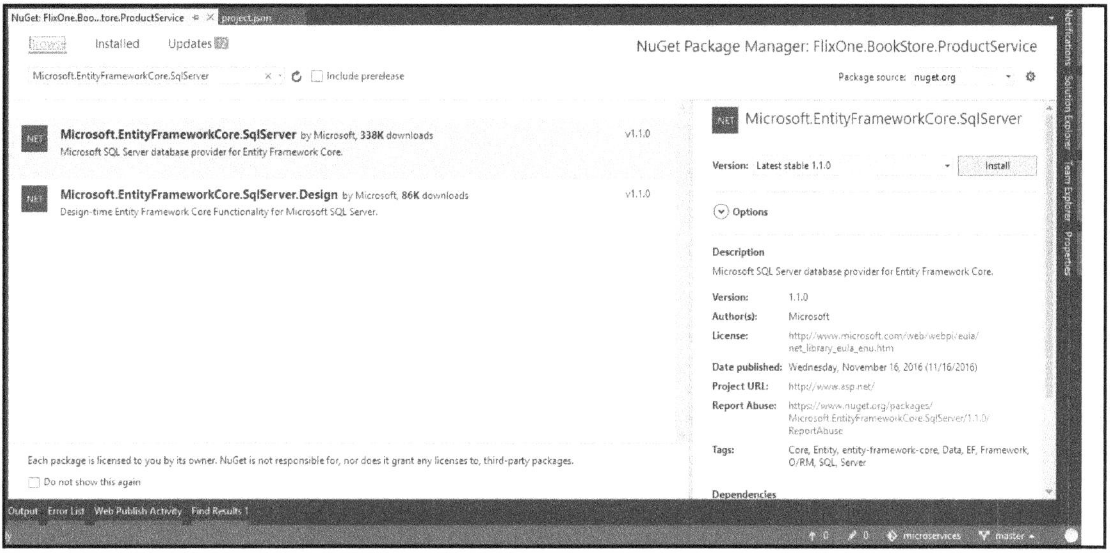

EF Core DbContext

In the preceding section, we added the EF Core package for SQL Server support; now we need to create a context so our models could interact with our product database. We have the Product and Category models. To do so, refer to this list:

- Add a new folder and name it `Contexts`--it is not compulsory to add a new folder
- In the `context` folder, add a new C# class and name it `ProductContext`--we are creating `DbContext` for ProductDatabase, so to make the similarity here, we are creating `ProductContext`
- Make sure the `ProductContext` class inherits the `DbContext` class
- Make the changes and our `ProductContext` class will look like this:

```
using FlixOne.BookStore.ProductService.Models;
using Microsoft.EntityFrameworkCore;
namespace FlixOne.BookStore.ProductService.Contexts
{
    public class ProductContext : DbContext
    {
        public ProductContext(DbContextOptions<ProductContext>
```

```
options): base(options)
        {       }
        public ProductContext()
        {       }
        public DbSet<Product> Products { get; set; }
        public DbSet<Category> Categories { get; set; }
    }
}
```

We have created our context, but this context is independent of Product database. We need to add a provider and connection string so that `ProductContext` can talk with our database.

- Once again open the `Startup.cs` file and add the SQL Server db provider for our EF Core support, under the `ConfigureServcies` method. Once you add the provider's `ConfigureServcies` method, our `Startup.cs` file will look like this:

```
public void ConfigureServices(IServiceCollection services)
{
        // Add framework services.
        services.AddMvc();
        services.AddSingleton<IProductRepository,
ProductRepository>();
    services.AddDbContext<ProductContext>(o =>

o.UseSqlServer(Configuration.GetConnectionString("ProductsConnection"
)));
    }
```

- Open the `appsettings.json` file and add the required database connection string. In our provider, we have already set the connection key as `ProductsConnection`. So now add the following line to set the connection string with the same key:

```
{
  "ConnectionStrings": {
    "ProductConnection":
      "Data Source=.SQLEXPRESS;Initial
Catalog=ProductsDB;Integrated
Security=True;MultipleActiveResultSets=True"
    }
  }
```

EF Core migrations

Although we have already created our product database, it is not time yet to underestimate the power of EF Core migrations. EF Core migrations will be helpful for us to perform any future modification to the database. This modification could be in the form of a simple field addition or any other update to the database structure. We can simply rely upon these EF Core migration commands every time to do the necessary changes for us. In order to utilize this capability, follow these simple steps:

1. Go to **Tools** | **NuGet Package Manager** | **Package Manager Console**.
2. Run the following commands from **Package Manager Console**:
   Install--Package `Microsoft.EntityFrameworkCore.Tools`--pre
   Install--Package `Microsoft.EntityFrameworkCore.Design`
3. To initiate the migration, run this command:
   Add-Migration ProductDB migration
   It is important to note that this is to be done only for the first time (when we do not yet have a database created by this command).
4. Now, whenever there are any changes in your model, simply execute the following command:
   Update-Database

Database migration

At this point, we are done with our ProductDatabase creation. Now its time to migrate our existing database. There are many different ways to do this. Our monolithic application, which presently has a huge database, contains a large number of records as well. It is not possible to migrate them by simply using a database SQL script.

We need to explicitly create a script to migrate the database with all of its data. Another option is to go ahead and create a DB package as required. Depending on the complexity of your data and the records, you might need to create more than one data package to ensure that the data is migrated correctly to our newly created database: `ProductDB`.

Revisiting repositories and the controller

We are now ready to facilitate interaction between our model and database via our newly created repositories. After making the appropriate changes to ProductRepository, it will look like this:

```
using System.Collections.Generic;
using System.Linq;
using FlixOne.BookStore.ProductService.Contexts;
using FlixOne.BookStore.ProductService.Models;
namespace FlixOne.BookStore.ProductService.Persistence
{
    public class ProductRepository : IProductRepository
    {
        private readonly ProductContext _context;
        public ProductRepository(ProductContext context)
        {
            _context = context;
        }
        public void Add(Product Product)
        {
            _context.Add(Product);
            _context.SaveChanges();
        }
        public IEnumerable<Product> GetAll()
        {
            return _context.Products.ToList();
        }
        //Rest of the code has been deleted
    }
}
```

Introducing ViewModel

Add a new class to the models folder and name it ProductViewModel--this is because in our monolithic application, whenever we search for a product, it should be displayed with its product category. In order to support this, we need to incorporate the necessary fields into our view model. Our ProductViewModel class will look like this:

```
using System;
namespace FlixOne.BookStore.ProductService.Models
{
    public class ProductViewModel
    {
        public Guid ProductId { get; set; }
```

```
        public string ProductName { get; set; }
        public string ProductDescription { get; set; }
        public string ProductImage { get; set; }
        public decimal ProductPrice { get; set; }
        public Guid CategoryId { get; set; }
        public string CategoryName { get; set; }
        public string CategoryDescription { get; set; }
    }
}
```

Revisiting the product controller

Finally, we are ready to create REST API for `ProductService`. After the changes are made, here is what `ProductController` will look like:

```
using System.Linq;
using FlixOne.BookStore.ProductService.Models;
using FlixOne.BookStore.ProductService.Persistence;
using Microsoft.AspNetCore.Mvc;
namespace FlixOne.BookStore.ProductService.Controllers
{
    [Route("api/[controller]")]
    public class ProductController : Controller
    {
        private readonly IProductRepository _ProductRepository;
        public ProductController(IProductRepository ProductRepository)
        {
            _ProductRepository = ProductRepository;
        }
        public IActionResult Get()
        {
            var Productvm = _ProductRepository.GetAll().Select(Product
=> new ProductViewModel
            {
                CategoryId = Product.CategoryId,
                CategoryDescription = Product.Category.Description,
                CategoryName = Product.Category.Name,
                ProductDescription = Product.Description,
                ProductId = Product.Id,
                ProductImage = Product.Image,
                ProductName = Product.Name,
                ProductPrice = Product.Price
            }).ToList();
            return new OkObjectResult(Productvm);
        }
        //Rest of code has been removed
```

```
        }
    }
```

Finally, we have completed the transition of our monolith .NET application to microservices in the process of discussing the step-by-step transition of ProductService. There are more steps to go with this application:

- How microservices communicate--this will be discussed in Chapter 3, *Integration Techniques*
- How to test a microservice-- this will be discussed in Chapter 4, *Testing Strategies*
- Deploying microservices--this will be discussed in Chapter 5, *Deployment*
- How can we make sure our microservices are secure and we monitor our microservices--this will be discussed in Chapter 6, *Security*, and Chapter 7, *Monitoring*
- How microservices are scaled--this will be discussed in Chapter 8, *Scaling*

Summary

In this chapter, we discussed different factors that can be used to identify and isolate microservices at a high level. We also discussed the various characteristics of a good service. Talking about DDD, we saw what its importance is in the context of microservices.

Further, we analyzed how we can correctly achieve vertical isolation of microservices through various parameters in detail. While we tried to draw upon our previous understanding of the challenges posed by a monolithic application and its solution in microservices, we saw that we can use factors such as module interdependency, technology utilization, and team structure to identify seams and perform the transition from a monolithic architecture to microservices in an organized manner.

It became apparent that the database can pose a clear challenge in the process. However, we identified how we can still perform this with a simple strategy and the possible approaches to do this. We then discussed that with the foreign keys reduced/removed, how the transactions are to be handled in a completely different manner.

Moving ahead from the requirement of dividing a monolith into bounded contexts, we further applied our knowledge to transition the FlixOne application to a microservice architecture.

3
Integration Techniques

In the previous chapter, we developed microservices using a .NET monolithic application. These services are independent of each other and are located on different servers. What would be a better way to have inter-service communication, where one service interacts/communicates with the other? In this chapter, we will discuss the various patterns and ways that will help us foster this communication. We will cover the following topics:

- Communication between services
- Styles of collaborations
- Integration patterns
- The API gateway
- The event-driven pattern
- Azure Service Bus

Communication between services

In the case of a .NET monolithic application, if there is a need to access third-party components or external services, we use the HTTP client or another client framework to access the resources. In `Chapter 2`, *Building Microservices*, we developed **Product service** in such a way that it would work independently. But this was not the case; we mandatorily required a few services to interact with each other. So this is a challenge: having services communicate with each other. Both **Product service** and **Order service** are hosted on separate servers. Both these servers are independent of each other, are based on **REST**, and have their own endpoints via which they communicate with each other (when a service interacts with another service and vice versa, we refer to it as inter-service communication as well).

There are ways in which services communicate with each other; let's discuss them briefly:

- **Synchronous**: In this, the client makes a request to the remote service (called a service) for a specific functionality and waits until it gets the response.

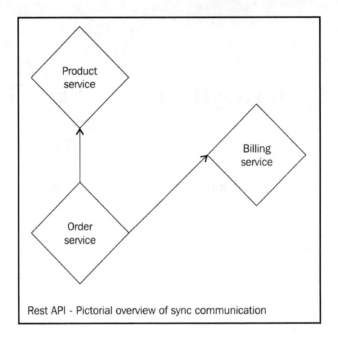

Rest API - Pictorial overview of sync communication

In the preceding image (pictorial view, not complete), you can see our different microservices communicate with each other. All our services are RESTful. They are based on the ASP.NET Core Web API. In the upcoming section, we will discuss this in detail: how exactly a service is called. This is known as the synchronous method, where clients have to wait for a response from the service. In this case, the client had to wait until it gets a complete response.

- **Asynchronous**: In this, clients make a request to the remote service (called a service) for a specific functionality and does not wait although it does care about the response. We will discuss this in detail in the following sections.

Styles of collaborations

In the preceding section, we discussed two different modes of how services intercommunicate. These modes are nothing but styles of collaborations, which are as follows:

- **request/response**: In this, the client sends a request and waits for the response from the server. This is an implementation of synchronous communication. But it is not true that request/response is only an implementation of synchronous communication; we can use it for asynchronous communication as well.

  Let's consider an example to understand the concept. In Chapter 2, *Building Microservices*, we developed ProductService. This service has the GetProduct method, which is synchronous. The client has to wait for a response whenever it calls this method:

```
    [HttpGet]
    [Route("GetProduct")]
    public IActionResult Get()
    {
        return new
OkObjectResult(_productRepository.GetAll().ToViewModel());
    }
```

  As per the preceding code snippet, whenever this method is called by the client (who is requesting for this), they will have to wait for the response, in other words, they will have to wait until the extension method ToViewModel() is executed:

```
  [HttpGet]
  [Route("GetProductSync")]
  public IActionResult GetIsStillSynchronous()
  {
          var task = Task.Run(async() => await
_productRepository.GetAllAsync());
          return new OkObjectResult(task.Result.ToViewModel());
  }
```

  In the preceding code snippet, we see that our method is implemented in such a way that whenever a client makes a request, they will have to wait until the async method is executed. Here, we call async in the sync way.

To make our code short, we added extension methods to the already existing code written in Chapter 2, *Building Microservices*:

```
using System.Collections.Generic;
using System.Linq;
using FlixOne.BookStore.ProductService.Models;

namespace FlixOne.BookStore.ProductService.Helpers.Extensions
{
    public static class Transpose
    {
        public static ProductViewModel ToViewModel(this Product
product)
        {
            return new ProductViewModel
            {
                CategoryId = product.CategoryId,
                CategoryDescription = product.Category.Description,
                CategoryName = product.Category.Name,
                ProductDescription = product.Description,
                ProductId = product.Id,
                ProductImage = product.Image,
                ProductName = product.Name,
                ProductPrice = product.Price
            };
        }
        public static IEnumerable<ProductViewModel>
ToViewModel(this IEnumerable<Product> products)
        {
            return products.Select(ToViewModel).ToList();
        }
    }
}
```

To sum up, we can say that the collaboration style request/response does not mean that it can be implemented only synchronously; we can use asynchronous calls for this as well.

- **Event-based**: The implementation of this collaborative style is purely asynchronous. This is a way of implementation where clients that emit an event do not know exactly how to react.

In the preceding section, we discussed **Product service** in a synchronous manner. Let's take an example of how users/customers can place an order; here is a pictorial overview of the functionality:

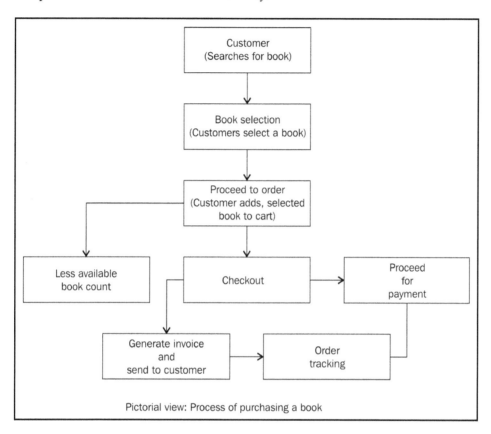

Pictorial view: Process of purchasing a book

The preceding figure shows that the process of purchasing a book has a few main functions:

1. With the help of the search functionality, customers can find a specific book.

2. After getting the results for the searched book, customers can view the details of the book.

3. As soon as they proceed to checkout, our system will make sure that the display (available books to purchase) would show the right quantity, for example, the available quantity is 10 copies of *Microservices for .NET* and the customer checks out with one book. In this case, the available quantity should now show nine copies.

4. The system will generate an invoice for the purchased book and send it to the customer on their registered e-mail.

Conceptually, this looks easy; however, when we talk about implementing microservices, we are taking about services that are hosted separately and have their own REST API, database and so on. This looks bit complex. There are many aspects involved, for example, how a service will call or invoke another service on a successful response from one or more services. This is where the event-driven architecture comes into the picture.

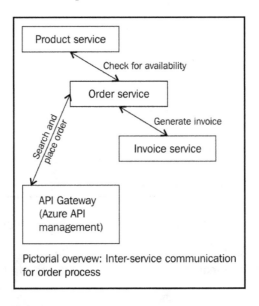

Pictorial overvew: Inter-service communication for order process

In the preceding image, we can see that `InvoiceService` and `ProductService` are triggered when `OrderService` is executed. These services further call internal asynchronous methods to complete their functionalities.

We are using Azure API management as our API gateway. In the upcoming sections, we will discuss this in detail.

Integration patterns

Until now, we have discussed inter-service communication and have gone through the practical implementation of **Product service** with the use of synchronous and asynchronous communication. We've also implemented microservices using different styles of collaborations. Our FlixOne bookstore (developed as per the microservice architectural style) required more interaction; therefore, it required more patterns. In this section, we will discuss the implementation of various integration patterns required for our application.

 The complete application of the FlixOne bookstore is available in `Chapter 10`, *Creating a Complete Microservice Solution.*

The API gateway

In the styles of collaboration section, we discussed two styles using which we can foster intercommunication between microservices. Our application is spread into various microservices:

- Product service
- Order service
- Invoice service
- Customer service

In our FlixOne bookstore (user interface), we need to show a few details:

- Book title, author name, price, discount, and so on
- Availability
- Book reviews
- Book ratings
- Publisher ranking and so on

Before we check out the implementation, let's discuss the API gateway.

The API gateway is nothing but an implementation of **Backend For Frontend (BFF)**. Sam Newman introduced this pattern. It acts as a proxy between client applications and services. In our example, we are using **Azure API management** as our API gateway.

It is responsible for the following functionalities:

- Accepting API calls and routes them to your backends
- Verifying API keys, JWT tokens, and certificates
- Supporting Auth through Azure AD and the OAuth 2.0 access token
- Enforcing usage quotas and rate limits
- Transforming your API on the fly without code modifications
- Caching backend responses wherever they are set up
- Logging call metadata for analytics purposes

 Refer to `Azure API management` to know more about the process of setting up the API Azure portal and working with REST APIs.

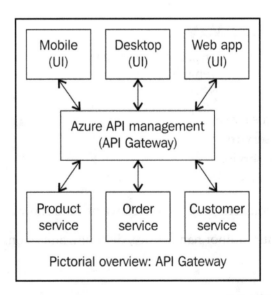

Pictorial overview: API Gateway

In the preceding image, we have different clients, such as a mobile and desktop application and a web application, that are using microservices. Here Azure API management is working as an API gateway. Our client does not know the actual server where our services are located. The API gateway provides them with the address of its own server, and internally, it authenticates the request from clients with the use of a valid `Ocp-Apim-Subscription-Key`.

Our `ProductService` has a REST API, refer to the following table:

API resource	Description
GET /api/product	Get a list of products
GET /api/product{id}	Get a product
PUT /api/product{id}	Update an existing product
DELETE /api/product{id}	Delete an existing product
POST /api/product	Add a new product

We have already created `ProductClient`--a .NET console application. It makes a request to Azure API management by passing the subscription key. Here is the code snippet for this:

```
namespace FlixOne.BookStore.ProductClient
{
    internal class Program
    {
        private const string ApiKey = "myAPI Key";
        private const string BaseUrl = "https://api.flixone.com";
        private static void Main(string[] args)
        {
            GetProductList("/product/GetProductSync");
            Console.WriteLine("Hit ENTER to exit...");
            Console.ReadLine();
        }
        private static async void GetProductList(string resource)
        {
            using (var client = new HttpClient())
            {
                var queryString =
HttpUtility.ParseQueryString(string.Empty);
                client.DefaultRequestHeaders.Add("Ocp-Apim-
Subscription-Key", ApiKey);
                var uri = $"{BaseUrl}{resource}?{queryString}";
                //Get asynchronous response for further usage
                var response = await client.GetAsync(uri);
            }
```

```
        }
      }
    }
```

In the preceding code, our client is requesting a REST API to get all the products. Here a brief description of the terms that appear in the code:

BaseUrl	**This is the address of the proxy server.**
Ocp-Apim-Subscription-Key	This is a key assigned by API Management to a specific product, which the client has opted for.
Resource	This is our API resource, which is configured over Azure API Management. It will be different from our actual Rest API resource.
Response	This refers to the response to a specific request, in our case, the default JSON format.

Since we're using Azure API Management as an API gateway, there are certain benefits we'll enjoy:

- We can manage our various APIs from a single platform; for example, `ProductService`, `OrderService`, and other services can be easily managed and called by many clients.
- Because we're using API management, it does not only provide us with a proxy server, but also provides the facility to create and maintain documentation of our APIs.
- It provides a built-in facility to define various policies for quota, output formats, and format conversions, such as XML to JSON or vice versa.

So with the help of the API gateway, we can have access to some great features.

The event-driven pattern

The microservice architecture has the database per service pattern, which means it has an independent database for every dependent or independent service:

- **Dependent service**: Our application would require a few external services (third-party services or components and so on) and/or internal services (these are our own services) to work or function as expected. For instance, **Checkoutservice** requires **Customer service**; also, **Checkout service** requires an external (third-party) service to verify a customer's identity (such as Aadhar card ID in the case of Indian customers). Here our **Checkoutservice** service is a dependent service, as it requires two (internal service and external service) services to function as expected. Dependent services would not work if any or all the services on which the service is dependent on do not work properly (there are a lot of causes due to which a service would not work, including network failure, unhandled exception, and so on).
- **Independent service**: In our application, we have services that do not require any other service to work properly. Services that do not need any other service to work in order to function are called independent services; these services can be self-hosted. Our **Cusomer service** does not require any other service to function properly, but other services may or may not require this service.

The main challenge is to maintain business transactions to ensure data consistency across these services. For instance, when and how **Customer service** would know that **CheckoutService** has functioned and now it requires the functionality of **Customer service**. There may be several services (services may be self-hosted) in an application. In our case, when **CheckoutService** is triggered and **Customer service** is not invoked, then how will our application identifies the customer's details?

 ASP.NET WebHooks can also be used for providing event notifications; refer to WebHooks documentation for more information.

To overcome the related problems/challenges we've discussed (for CheckoutService and CustomerService), we can use an event-driven pattern (or the eventual consistency approach) and use distributed transactions.

A distributed transaction is a transaction that updates data on two or more networked computer systems. Distributed transactions extend the benefits of transactions to applications that must update distributed data. Implementing robust distributed applications is difficult because these applications are subject to multiple failures, including failure of the client, the server, and the network connection between the client and server. In the absence of distributed transactions, the application program itself must detect and recover from these failures. - msdn

The following image describes an actual implementation of the event-driven pattern in our application, where ProductService subscribes to the events and **Event-Manager** manages all the events:

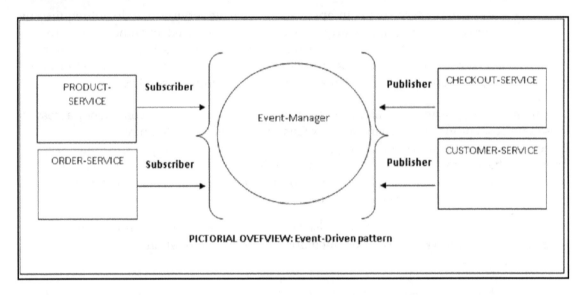

PICTORIAL OVEFVIEW: Event-Driven pattern

In an event-driven pattern, we implement a service in such a way that it publishes an event whenever a service updates its data and another service (dependent service) subscribes to this event. Now whenever a dependent service receives an event, it updates its data. This way, our dependent services can get and update their data as/if required. The preceding image shows an overview of how services subscribe to and publish events. In the image, **Event-Manger** could be a program running on a service or a mediator helping you manage all the events of the subscribers and publishers. It registers an event of the publisher and notifies it to a subscriber whenever a specific event is occurred/triggered. It also helps you to form a queue and wait for events. In our implementation, we will use Azure Service Bus queues for this activity.

Let's consider an example. In our application, this is how our services will publish and receive an event:

1. **CustomerService** performs a few checks for the users, namely login check, customer details check, and so on; after these necessary checks are conducted, the service publishes an event called **CustomerVerified**.
2. CheckOutService receives this event and after performing the necessary operations, it publishes an event called ReadyToCheckout.
3. **Order-Service** receives this event and updates the quantity.
4. As soon as the checkout is performed, CheckOutService publishes an event. Whatever result is received from the external service, either CheckedoutSuccess or CheckedoutFailed, it is used by CheckoutService.
5. When InventoryService receives these events, it updates the data to make sure the exact item is added or removed.

With the use of event-driven patterns, services can automatically update the database and publish an event.

Event sourcing

This pattern helps us ensure that the service will publish an event whenever the state changes. In this pattern, we take a business entity (product, customer, and so on) as a sequence of state-changing events. The event store persists the events and these events are available for subscription or as other services. This pattern simplifies our tasks by avoiding the requirement to synchronize the data model and the business domain. It improves performance, scalability, and responsiveness.

- This simply defines an approach indicating how we can handle the various operations on our data by a sequence of events; these events are recorded in a store.

- An event represents a set of changes made to the data, for example, InvoiceCreated.

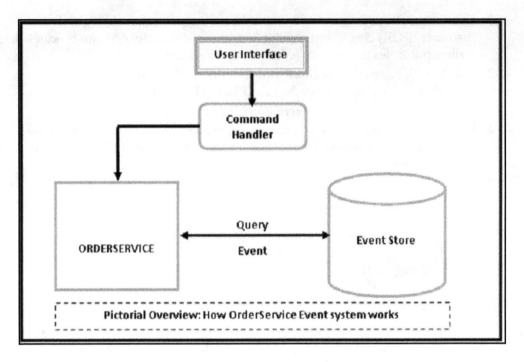

Pictorial Overview: How OrderService Event system works

The preceding image describes how an event would work for Orderservice:

- The commands issue a book from the UI to Order.
- OrderService queries (from the event store) and populates the results with the CreateOrder event.
- Then, the command handler raises an event to order the book.
- Our service performs the related operations.
- Finally, the system appends the event to the event store.

Eventual consistency

Eventual consistency is nothing but an implementation of the data consistency approach. This suggests implementation so, the system would be a scalable system with high availability.

> *Eventual consistency is unlikely to be specified as an explicit requirement of a distributed system. Instead it is often a result of implementing a system that must exhibit scalability and high availability, which precludes most common strategies for providing strong consistency* - msdn

According to this distributed data, stores are subject to the CAP theorem. The CAP theorem is also known as Brewer's theorem. Consistency, Availability, (network) Partition tolerance (CAP). According to this theorem, in a distributed system, we can only choose two out of these three:

- Consistency
- Availability
- Partition tolerance

Compensating Transaction

Compensating Transactions provide a way to roll back or undo all the tasks performed in a step of series. Suppose one or more services have implemented operations in a series and one or more of them have failed. What would be your next steps then? Would you reverse all the steps or commit to a half-completed functionality?

In our case, where a customer orders a book and ProductService marks the ordered book as sold temporarily, after the confirmation of the order, OrderService calls an external service for completing the payment process. If the payment fails, we would need to undo our previous tasks, which means we will have to check ProductService so it would mark the specific book as unsold.

Competing Consumers

Competing Consumers provides a way to process messages for multiple concurrent consumers, where they receive these messages on the same channel. This application is meant for handling a large number of requests. It can be implemented by passing a messaging system to another service (a consumer service), and it can be handled asynchronously.

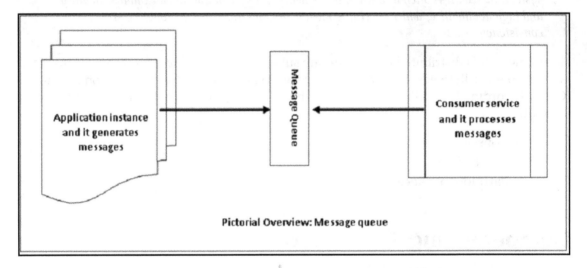

Pictorial Overview: Message queue

This scenario can be implemented with the use of Azure Service Bus queues.

Azure Service Bus queues

In the event-driven pattern, we discussed services' publish and subscribe events. We used an event manager to manage all the events. In this section, we will see how Azure Service Bus manages events and provides the facility to work with microservices.

Azure Service Bus is nothing but an information delivery service. It is used to make communication easier between two or more components/services. In our case, whenever services need to exchange information, they will communicate using this. Azure Service Bus plays an important role here. There are two main types of services provided by Azure Service Bus:

- **Brokered communication** – This service can also be called hired service. It works in the similar way as postal services work in our real world. Whenever a person wants to send message/information, he/she can send a letter to another person. This way, one can send various types of messages in the form of letters, packages, gifts, and so on. This type of messaging service ensures delivery of a message even when both the sender and receiver are not online at the same time. This is a messaging platform with components such as queues, topics and subscriptions, and so on.

- **Non-brokered communication** – This is similar to making a phone call. In this, the caller (sender) calls a person (receiver) without any confirmation indicating whether he/she will pick the call or not. In this, the sender sends information and it purely depends upon the receiver to receive the communication and pass the message back to the sender.

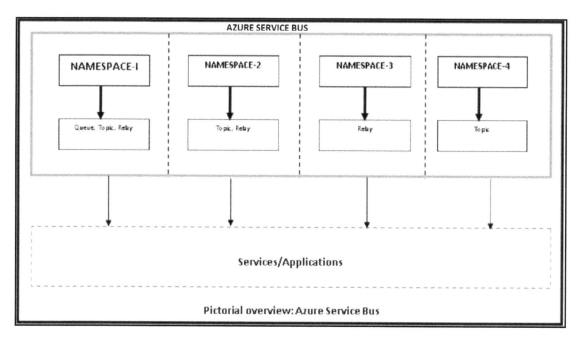

Pictorial overview: Azure Service Bus

> *Service Bus is a multi-tenant cloud service, which means that the service is shared by multiple users. Each user, such as an application developer, creates a namespace, then defines the communication mechanisms she needs within that namespace* - msdn

The preceding image is a pictorial view of Azure Service Bus and it depicts four different communication mechanisms. Everyone has own taste via which it connects application.

- **Queues** – These allow one-directional communication and act as brokers.
- **Topics** – These provide one-directional communication where a single topic can have multiple subscriptions.
- **Relays** – These provide bi-directional communication. They do not store messages (as queues and topics do). Relays pass messages to the destination application.

Implementation of an Azure Service Bus queue

In this section, we will see the actual implementation of an Azure Service Bus queue by creating the following:

- A Service Bus namespace
- A Service Bus messaging queue
- A console application to send a message
- A console application to receive a message

Prerequisites

We need the following to implement this solution:

- Visual Studio 2015 Update 3 or later
- A valid Azure subscription

If you do not have any Azure subscription, you can get it for free by signing in here: https://azure.microsoft.com/en-us/free/

If you have everything, as mentioned, you can start by following these steps:

1. Log on to the Azure portal (`https://portal.azure.com/`).
2. In the left navigation bar, click on **Service Bus**--if unavailable, you can find it by clicking on **More Services.**
3. Click on **Add**.

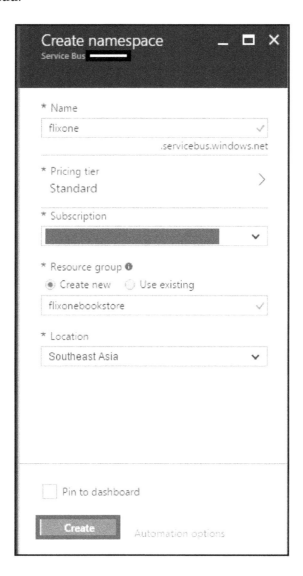

4. In the **Create namespace** dialog, enter a namespace, say `flixone`. Select the pricing tier next: `Basic,` `Standard,` or `Premium` .
5. Select your subscription.
6. Choose an existing resource or create a new one.
7. Select the location where you want to host the namespace
8. Open a newly created namespace (we just created `flixone`)
9. Now click on **Shared access policies**.
10. Click on **RootManageSharedAccessKey:**

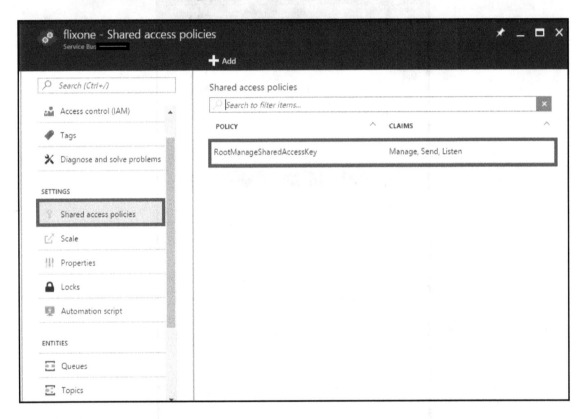

11. Click on **Queues** in the main dialog of the `flixone` namespace.

12. From the Policy: RootManageSharedAccessKey window, note the primary key connection string for further use.

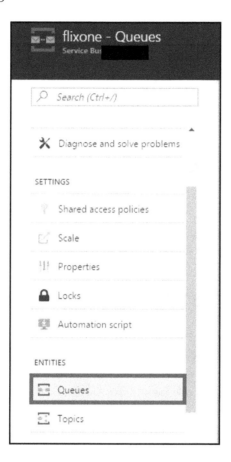

13. Click on **Add Queue name** (say flixonequeue) and click on **Create** (we're using rest values as default values):

You can verify the creation of the queue by visiting the Queues dialog.

Now we are ready to create our sender and receiver applications for messages.

Sending messages to the queue

In this section, we will create a console application that will actually send messages to the queue. To create this application, follow these steps:

1. Create a new console application and name it **FlixOne.BookStore.MessageSender** using Visual Studio's new project (C#) template:

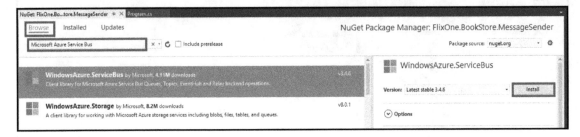

2. Add the Nuget package **Microsoft Azure Service Bus** by right-clicking on the project.

3. Open the `app.config` file and add the connection string and queue name.

```
<appSettings>
        <!-- Service Bus specific app settings for messaging
connections -->
            <add
key="Microsoft.ServiceBus.ConnectionString"
value="Endpoint=sb://flixone.servicebus.windows.net/;SharedAccessKeyN
ame=RootManageSharedAccessKey;SharedAccessKey=sharedprimarykey"/>
            <add key="FlixOneQueueName" value="flixonequeue"/>
</appSettings>
```

4. Add a reference of **System.Configuration.**

5. Write the code to send the message to the queue, and your `Program.cs` file will look like this:

```
using System.Configuration;
using Microsoft.ServiceBus.Messaging;
namespace FlixOne.BookStore.MessageSender
{
    internal class Program
    {
        private static void Main(string[] args)
        {
            var connectionString =
```

```
ConfigurationManager.AppSettings["Microsoft.ServiceBus.ConnectionStri
ng"];
            var queueName =
ConfigurationManager.AppSettings["FlixOneQueueName"];
            var client =
QueueClient.CreateFromConnectionString(connectionString,
queueName);         var message = new BrokeredMessage("A message
from FlixOne.BookStore.MessageSender");
client.Send(message);
        }
    }
}
```

6. Run the program and wait for a while.
7. Go to the created queue and check whether it displays a message:

Receiving messages from the queue

In this section, we will create a console application that would receive messages from the queue. To create this application, follow these steps:

1. Create a new console application (C#) and name it `FlixOne.BookStore.MessageReceiver`.
2. Add the NuGet package for Azure Service Bus (same as added in the previous application).
3. Add config keys/values to your `App.Config` file and a reference of `System.Configuration` to the project.
4. Write the code to receive messages from the Azure Bus Service queue, so your `program.cs` file should look like this:

```
using System;
using System.Configuration;
using Microsoft.ServiceBus.Messaging;
namespace FlixOne.BookStore.MessageReceiver
{
    internal class Program
    {
        private static void Main(string[] args)
        {
            var connectionString =
ConfigurationManager.AppSettings["Microsoft.ServiceBus.ConnectionStri
ng"];
            var queueName =
ConfigurationManager.AppSettings["QueueName"];
            var client =
QueueClient.CreateFromConnectionString(connectionString,
queueName);            client.OnMessage(message =>
            {
                Console.WriteLine($"Message:
{message.GetBody<string>()}");
                Console.WriteLine($"Message id: {message.MessageId}");
            });
            Console.ReadLine();
        }
    }
}
```

Note that we have sent one message to our Azure Bus Service queue.

Now, run the application and see the result.

```
Message: A message from FlixOne.BookStore.MessageSender
Message id: 9f05a43eaa3a4cf48039b5d290540461
```

The console window will display the message and its ID. Now go to the Azure portal and verify the message. It should be zero:

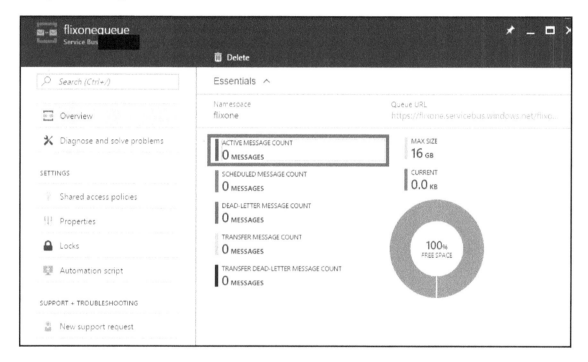

The preceding example demonstrates how we can use Azure Bus Service to send/receive messages for our microservices.

Summary

Inter-service communication is possible with synchronous or asynchronous communication, which are styles of collaborations. Microservices should have asynchronous APIs. The API gateway is a proxy server that provides a way to interact various clients with APIs. API management, as an API gateway, provides plenty of features to manage/host various RESTful APIs. There are various patterns that help us communicate with microservices. With the use of Azure Bus Service, we can easily manage and play with inter-service communication using the Azure Bus Service message queue; services can easily send or receive messages from each other through this. Eventual consistency talks about scalable systems with high scalability, and it is proven with the CAP theorem.

In the next chapter, we will discuss various testing strategies to test an application and build on the microservice architectural style.

4
Testing Strategies

Quality assurance or testing is a great way to assess a system, program, or an application with different aspects. Sometimes, a system requires testing to identify erroneous code; on other occasions, we may need it to assess our system's business compliance. Testing could vary from system to system and can be considerably different as per the architectural style of the application. Everything depends on how we are strategizing our testing approach or plan; for example, testing a monolith .NET application will be different as compared to testing SOA or microservices. In this chapter, we will cover these topics:

- How to test microservices
- Handling challenges
- Testing strategies
- The testing pyramid
- Types of microservice tests

How to test microservices

Testing microservices could be a challenging job as it is different from how we test applications built using the traditional architectural style. In a .NET monolithic application, testing is a bit easier compared to microservices, which provides implementation independence and short delivery cycles.

Let's understand it in the context of our .NET monolithic application, where we did not utilize continuous integration and deployment. It becomes more complex when testing is combined with continuous integration and deployment. In microservices, we will be required to understand the tests for every service and how these tests differ from each other. Also, note that automated testing does not mean that we will not perform any manual testing at all.

Here are a few things that make microservice testing a complex and challenging task:

- Microservices might have multiple services that work together or individually for an enterprise system, so they can be complex.
- Microservices are meant to target multiple clients, hence they involve more complex use cases.
- Each component/service of the microservice architectural style is isolated and independent, so it is a bit complex to test them as they need to be tested individually and as a complete system.
- There might be independent teams working on separate components/services, which might be required to interact with each other; therefore, they should be tested in a way that the tests would cover not only internal but also external services. This makes the job of testing microservices more challenging and complex.
- In microservices, each component/service is designed to work independently, but they might be common for various other services and have a requirement to access common/shared data. But in microservices, each service is responsible for modifying its own database. So, testing microservices is going to be more complex as services would now need to access data using API calls with other services, which further adds dependencies to other services. This type of testing will have to be handled using mock tests.

Handling challenges

In the previous section, we discussed that testing a microservice is a complex and challenging job. In this section, we will discuss some points that will indicate how conducting various tests could help us overcome these challenges:

- A unit test framework, such as Microsoft Unit Testing Framework, provides a facility to test individual operations of independent components. To ensure that all the tests pass and that a new functionality or change does not break anything (if any functionality breaks down, then the related unit test would fail), these tests can be run on every compilation of code.

- To make sure that responses are consistent with the expectations of the clients or consumers, consumer-driven contract testing can be used.
- Services use data from an external party or from other services, and they can be tested by setting up the endpoint of the services that are responsible for handling the data. Then we can use mocking framework or library such as `moq` to mock these endpoints during the integration process.

Testing strategies (testing approach)

As mentioned in the prerequisites section of `Chapter 1`, *What are Microservices?*, deployment and QA requirements would become more demanding. The only way to effectively handle this scenario would be through preemptive planning. I have always favored the representation of the QA team during the early requirement gathering and design phase. In the case of microservices, it becomes a necessity to have a close collaboration between the architecture group and the QA group. Not only would the QA group input be helpful, but the QA group would be able to draw up a strategy to test the microservices effectively.

Test strategies are nothing but a map or outlined plan that describes the complete approach of testing.

Different systems require different testing approaches. It is not possible to implement a pure testing approach to a system that is developed using a newer approach rather than the earlier developed system. Testing strategies should be clear to everyone so that the created tests can help non-technical members of the team (such as stakeholders) understand how the system is working. Such tests can be automated, which simply tests the business flow, or they could be manual tests which could be simply performed by a user working on the User Acceptance Testing system.

Testing strategies or approaches have the following techniques:

- **Proactive** – This is kind of an early approach and tries to fix defects at the earliest before the build is created by the initiated test designs.
- **Reactive** – In this approach, testing is started or comes into the picture once coding is completed.

Testing pyramid

The testing pyramid is a strategy or a way to define what you should test in microservices. In other words, we can say it helps us define the testing scope of microservices. The concept of the testing pyramid was originated by *Mike Cohn* (`http://www.mountaingoatsoftware.com/blog/the-forgotten-layer-of-the-test-automation-pyramid`) in 2009. There are various flavors of the testing pyramid; different authors have described this by indicating how they had placed or prioritized their testing scope. The following image depicts the same concept that was defined by Mike Cohn:

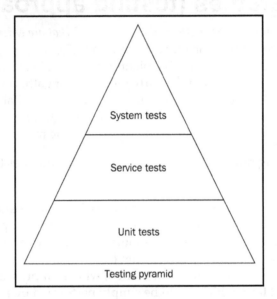

The **Testing pyramid** showcases how a well-designed test strategy is structured. When we closely look at it, we can easily notice how we should follow the testing approach for microservices (note that the testing pyramid is not specific to microservices). Let's start from the bottom of this pyramid. We can see that the testing scope is very limited with the use of **Unit tests**. As soon as we move to the top, our testing scope is expanded into a broader scope where we can perform complete system testing.

Let's talk about these layers in detail (bottom-to-top approach):

- **Unit tests**: These are tests that test small functionalities of an application based on the microservice architectural style.
- **Service tests**: These are tests that test an independent service or a service that could communicate with another/external service.
- **System tests**: These are tests that help in testing an entire system with the aspect of the user interface. These are end-to-end tests.

One interesting point in this concept is the top-layered tests, that is, system tests, are slow and expensive to write and maintain. On the other hand, the bottom-layered tests, that is, unit tests, are comparatively fast and less expensive.

In the upcoming sections, we will discuss these tests in detail.

Types of microservice tests

In the previous section, we discussed test approaches or testing strategies. These strategies decide how we will proceed with the testing of the system. In this section, we will discuss various types of microservice testing.

Unit testing

Unit tests are tests that typically test a single function call to ensure that the smallest piece of the program is tested. So these tests are meant to verify specific functionality without considering other components:

- Testing would be more complex when components are broken down into small, independent pieces and that are supposed to be tested independently. Here, testing strategies come in handy and ensure that the best quality assurance of a system would be performed. It adds more power when it comes along with the **Test-Driven Development (TDD)** approach.
- Unit tests are of any size, or say, there is no definition for the size of unit tests. Generally, these tests are written at the class level.
- Smaller unit tests are good to test every possible functionality of a complex system.

Component (service) testing

Component or service testing is a method where we bypass the UI and directly test the API (in our case, the ASP.NET Core Web API). Using this test, we confirm that an individual service does not have any code bugs or that it is working fine functionality-wise.

Testing a service does not mean it is an independent service. This service might be interacting with an external service. In such a scenario, we should not call the actual service but use the mock and stub approach. The reason for this is our motto to test code and make sure it is bug-free. In our case, we will use the `moq` framework for mocking our services.

There are a few things worth to be noted in the case of component or service testing:

- As we need to verify the functionality of the services, these kinds of tests could be small and fast.
- With the help of mocking, we don't need to deal with the actual database; therefore, test execution time is less or nominally higher.
- The scope of these tests is broader than unit tests.

Integration testing

In unit testing, we test a single unit of code. In component or service testing, we test mock services depending on an external or third-party component. But integration testing in microservices is a bit challenging or critical as in this type of testing, we test components that work together; also, service calls here should be made with integration with external services. In this test strategy, we make sure that the system is working together correctly and the behavior of services are as expected. In our case, we have various microservices and some of them depend upon external services.

For example, StockService depends upon OrderService in a way that a particular number of items is reduced from the stock as soon as the customer successfully orders that specific item. In this scenario, when we test StockService, we should mock OrderService. Our motto should be to test StockService and not communicate with OrderService. We do not test directly with the database of any service.

Contract testing

Contract testing is an approach where each service calls independently verifies the response. If any service is dependent, then dependencies are stubbed. This way, the service functions without interacting with any other service. This is an integration test that allows us to check the contract of external services. Here we come to a concept called the consumer-driven contract (we will discuss this in detail in the following section).

For example, **CustomerService** allows new customers to register with the FlixOne Store. We do not store new customers' data in our database. We verify customer data before this to check for blacklisting or fraud user listing and so on. This process calls an external service that is maintained by another team or entirely by a third-party. Out tests will still pass if someone changes the contract of this external service because this change would not affect our test, as we stubbed the contract of this external service.

Consumer-driven contracts

In microservices, we have several services that are independent or services that require communication with each other. Apart from this, from a user's (here, the user is a developer, who is consuming the API being referred to) point of view, they know about the service and whether it has or doesn't have several clients/consumers/users. These clients can have the same or different needs.

Consumer-driven contracts refer to a pattern that specifies and verifies all the interactions between clients/consumers and the API owner (application). So here, consumer-driven means that the client/consumer specifies what kind of interactions it is asking for with the defined format. On the other hand, the API owner (application services) must then agree to these contracts and ensure that they are not breaking them:

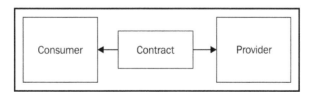

These are the contracts:

- **Provider contract:** This is nothing but a complete description of the service provided by the API owner (application). Swagger's documentation can be used for our REST API (web API).
- **Consumer contract:** This is nothing but a description of how consumers/clients are going to utilize the Provider contract.
- **Consumer-driven contract:** This is nothing but a description of how the API owner satisfies consumer/client contracts.

How to implement a consumer-driven test

In the case of microservices, it's a bit challenging/harder to implement a consumer-driven test instead of a .NET monolithic application. This is because in monolithic applications, we can directly use any unit test framework, such as MS tests or NUnit, but we can't do this directly in the microservice architecture. In microservices, we would need to mock not only method calls, but also the services themselves, which get called via either HTTP or HTTPs.

To implement a consumer-driven test, there are tools available that will help. One famous open source tool for .NET framework is *Pact-ne*t (`https://github.com/SEEK-Jobs/pact-net`) and another for .NET Core is *Pact-net*-core (`https://github.com/garora/pact-net-core`). These are based on *Pact* (`https://docs.pact.io/`) standards.

How Pact-net-core helps us achieve our goal

In a consumer-driven test, our goal is to make sure that we should be able to test all the services, internal components, and services that depend on or communicate with other/external services.

Pact-net-core is written in a way that it guarantees the contacts would be met. Here are a few points on how it helps us in a better way to achieve our goal:

- The execution is very fast
- It helps identify failure causes
- The main thing is that Pact does not require a separate environment to manage automation test integration.

There are two steps to work with Pact:

- **Defining expectations:** In the very first step, the consumer team has to define the contract. In the preceding image, Pact helps record the consumer contract, which will be verified when replayed:

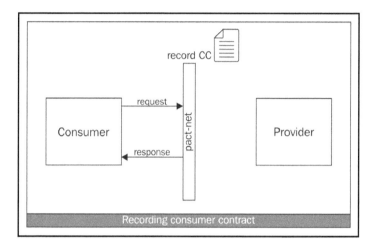

- **Verifying expectations** – As part of the next step, the contract is provided to the provider team and then the provider service is implemented to fulfill the same. In the following image, we are showing the replaying of a contract on the provider side to fulfill the defined contract.

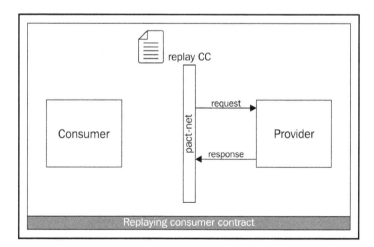

We have gone through consumer-driven contracts; they mitigate our challenges of microservice architectures with the help of an open source tool called Pact-net.

Performance testing

This is non-functional testing, and its main motto is not to verify the code or test the code health. This is meant to ensure that the system is performing well, based on the various measures, namely scalability, reliability, and so on.

The following are the different techniques or types of performance testing:

- **Load testing**: This is nothing but a process where we test the behavior of the system under various circumstances of specific load. It also covers critical transactions, database load, application server, and so on.
- **Stress testing**: This is an approach where the system goes under regress testing and finds the upper limit capacity of the system. It is also determined by how a system behaves in this critical situation, where the current load goes above the expected maximum load.
- **Soak testing**: This is also called endurance testing. In this test, the main purpose is to monitor memory utilizations, memory leaks, or various factors that affect the system performance.
- **Spike testing**: This is an approach where we make sure that the system is able to sustain the workload. One of the best tasks to determine performance is by suddenly increasing the user load.

End-to-end (UI/functional) testing

End-to-end or UI or functional tests are those that perform for the entire system, including the entire service and database integration. These tests increase the scope of testing. It is the highest level of testing and includes frontend integration and tests the system as an end user would use it. This testing is somehow similar to the end user working with the system.

Sociable versus isolated unit tests

Sociable unit tests are those that contain concrete collaborators and cross boundaries. They are not solitary tests. Solitary tests are those that ensure that the methods of a class are tested. Sociable testing is not new. This word is explained in detail by Martin Fowler as a unit test (`https://martinfowler.com/bliki/UnitTest.html`):

- **Sociable tests**: This is nothing but a test that lets us know the application is working as expected. This is the environment where other applications behave correctly, run smoothly, and produce the expected results. It also, somehow, tests the functioning of new functions/methods, including other software for the same environment. Sociable tests resemble system testing because these tests behave like system tests.
- **Isolated unit tests**: As the name suggests, you can use this to perform unit testing in an isolated way by performing stubbing and mocking. We can perform unit testing with a concrete class using stubs.

Stubs and mocks

Stubs are nothing but returned canned responses to calls made during the test; mocks are meant to set expectations:

- **Stubs**: In a stubs object, we always get a valid stubbed response. The response doesn't care what input you provide. In any circumstances, the output will be the same.
- **Mocks**: In a mock object, we can test or validate methods that can be called on mocked objects. This is a fake object that validates whether a unit test has failed or passed. In other words, we can say that mock objects are just a replica of our actual object. In the following code, we use the `moq` framework to implement a mocked object:

```
[Fact]
public void Get_Returns_ActionResults()
{
    // Arrange
    var mockRepo = new Mock<IProductRepository>();
    mockRepo.Setup(repo =>
repo.GetAll().ToViewModel()).Returns(GetProducts());
    var controller = new ProductController(mockRepo.Object);
    // Act
    var result = controller.Get();
    // Assert
```

```
        var viewResult = Assert.IsType<OkObjectResult>(result);
        var model =
Assert.IsAssignableFrom<IEnumerable<ProductViewModel>>(viewResult.Value);
        Assert.Equal(2, model.Count());
}
```

In the preceding code example, we mocked our `IProductRepository` repository and verified the mocked result.

In the upcoming sections, we will understand these terms in more detail, using more code examples from our FlixOne bookstore application.

Tests in action

Until now, we have discussed test strategies and various types of microservice tests. We've also discussed how to test and what to test. In this section, we will see tests in action; we will implement tests with the use of:

- Visual Studio 2017 RC or later
- .NET Core
- ASP.NET Core API
- xUnit and MS tests
- The Moq framework

Getting ready with the test project

We will test our microservice application: FlixOne bookstore. With the help of code examples, we will see how to perform unit tests, stubbing, and mocking.

 We created the FlixOne bookstore application in `Chapter 2`, *Building Microservices*.

Before we start writing tests, we should set up a test project in our existing application. There are a few simple steps we can take with this test project setup:

- Using Visual Studio, add a new .NET Core (class library) project to your existing solution
- You can alternatively use the `cli` command to add the new project--open the bash command or the Visual Studio command prompt and execute `dotnet new -t xunittest`
- Open the `project.json` file of your test project and make sure these dependencies and packages are there:

```
{
  "version": "1.0.0-*",
  "buildOptions": {
    "debugType": "portable"
  },
  "dependencies": {
    "System.Runtime.Serialization.Primitives": "4.1.1",
    "xunit": "2.1.0",
    "dotnet-test-xunit": "1.0.0-rc2-192208-24",
    "FlixOne.BookStore.ProductService": { "target": "project" },
    "Microsoft.AspNetCore.TestHost": "1.1.0"
  },
  "testRunner": "xunit",
  "frameworks": {
    "netcoreapp1.0": {
      "dependencies": {
        "Microsoft.NETCore.App": {
          "type": "platform",
          "version": "1.0.1"
        }
      },
      "imports": [
        "dotnet5.4",
        "portable-net451+win8"
      ]
    }
  }
}
```

Our project structure should look like this:

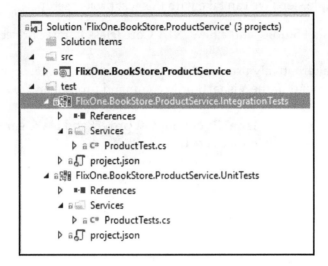

Unit tests

In `ProductService`, let's make sure that our service returns product data without failure:

```
namespace FlixOne.BookStore.ProductService.Tests.Services
{
    public class ProductTests
    {
        private IEnumerable<ProductViewModel> GetProducts()
        {
            var productVm = new List<ProductViewModel>
            {
                new ProductViewModel
                {
                    CategoryId = Guid.NewGuid(),
                    CategoryDescription = "Category Description",
                    CategoryName = "Category Name",
                    ProductDescription = "Product Description",
                    ProductId = Guid.NewGuid(),
                    ProductImage = "Image full path",
                    ProductName = "Product Name",
                    ProductPrice = 112M
                },
                new ProductViewModel
                {
                    CategoryId = Guid.NewGuid(),
```

```
                    CategoryDescription = "Category Description-01",
                    CategoryName = "Category Name-01",
                    ProductDescription = "Product Description-01",
                    ProductId = Guid.NewGuid(),
                    ProductImage = "Image full path",
                    ProductName = "Product Name-01",
                    ProductPrice = 12M
                }
            };
            return productVm;
        }
        [Fact]
        public void Get_Returns_ActionResults()
        {
            // Arrange
            var mockRepo = new Mock<IProductRepository>();
            mockRepo.Setup(repo =>
repo.GetAll().ToViewModel()).Returns(GetProducts());
            var controller = new ProductController(mockRepo.Object);
            // Act
            var result = controller.Get();
            // Assert
            var viewResult = Assert.IsType<OkObjectResult>(result);
            var model =
Assert.IsAssignableFrom<IEnumerable<ProductViewModel>>
(viewResult.Value);
            Assert.Equal(2, model.Count());
        }
    }
  }
```

In the preceding code example, which is a unit test example, we are mocking our repository and testing the output of our WebAPI controller. This test is based on the *AAA* technique; it will be passed if you meet the mocked data during setup.

Integration tests

In `ProductService`, let's make sure that our service returns the product data without failure:

```
namespace FlixOne.BookStore.ProductService.IntegrationTests.Services
{
    public class ProductTest
    {
        public ProductTest()
        {
            // Arrange
            _server = new TestServer(new WebHostBuilder()
                .UseStartup<Startup>());
            _client = _server.CreateClient();
            _client.BaseAddress = new Uri("http://localhost:20077");
        }
        private readonly HttpClient _client;
        private readonly TestServer _server;
        [Fact]
        public async Task ReturnHelloWorld()
        {
            // Act
            var response = await _client.GetAsync("/GetProduct");
            response.EnsureSuccessStatusCode();
            var responseString = await
    response.Content.ReadAsStringAsync();
            // Assert
            Assert.NotEmpty(responseString);
        }
    }
}
```

In the preceding code example, we are checking a simple test, where we are trying to verify the response of a service by setting up a client with the use of `HttpClient`. The test will fail if the response goes empty.

Summary

Testing microservices is a bit different from applications built on the traditional architectural style. In a .NET monolithic application, testing is a bit easier as compared to microservices, and it provides implementation independence and short delivery cycles. Microservices face challenges while performing the testing. With the help of the testing pyramid concept, we can strategize how to go with testing. Referring to the testing pyramid, we can easily see that unit tests provide the facility to test a small function of a class and are less time-consuming. On the other hand, the top layer of the testing pyramid enters a large scope with system or end-to-end testing, and these tests are time taking and much expensive. Consumer-driven contracts are a very useful way to test microservices. Pact-net is an open source tool meant for this. Finally, we went through the actual test implementation.

In the next chapter, we will see how to deploy a microservice application. We will discuss continuation integration and continuation deployment in detail.

5
Deployment

Both monolith and microservice architectural styles come with different deployment challenges. In the case of .NET monolithic applications, more often, deployments are a flavor of xcopy deployments. Microservice deployments present a different set of challenges. Continuous integration and continuous deployment are the key practices to deliver microservice applications. Also, container technologies and their toolchain to build and deploy, which promises greater isolation boundaries, are essential for microservice deployment and scaling.

In this chapter, we will discuss the fundamentals of microservice deployment and the influence of emerging practices, such as CI/CD tools and containers, on microservice deployment. We will also walk through the deployment of a simple .NET Core service into a Docker container.

By the end of the chapter, you will have an understanding of the following topics:

- Deployment terminology
- What are the factors for successful microservice deployments?
- What is continuous integration and continuous deployment?
- Isolation requirements for microservice deployment
- Containerization technology and its need for microservice deployment
- Quick introduction to docker
- How to package an application as a docker container using Visual Studio

Monolithic application deployment challenges

Monolithic applications are applications where all of the database and business logic is tied together and packaged as a single system. Since, in general, monolithic applications are deployed as a single package, deployments are somewhat simple but painful due to the following reasons:

- **Deployment and release as a single concept:** There is no differentiation between deploying build artifacts and actually making features available to the end user. More often, releases have coupling to the environments. This increases the risk of deploying new features.

- **All or nothing deployment:** All or nothing deployment increases the risk of application downtime and failures. In the case of rollbacks, teams fail to deliver the expected new features. Besides, hotfixes, or service packs become the norm to deliver the right kind of functionality.

- **Central databases as a single point of failure:** In monolithic applications, a big, centralized database is a single point of failure. This database is quite often large and difficult to break down. This results in an increase in **mean time to recover (MMTR)** and **mean time between failures (MTBF)**.

- **Deployment and releases are big events:** Due to small changes in the application, the entire application could get deployed. This comes with developers and ops teams' huge time and energy investment. Needless to say, collaboration between the various teams involved is the key for a successful release. This becomes even harder when many geo-distributed teams are working on the development and release. These kinds of deployments/releases use a lot of handholding and manual steps. This impacts the end customers who have to face application downtime. If you are familiar with these kinds of deployments, then you'll also be familiar with marathon sessions in the so-called war rooms and endless sessions of defect triage on conference bridges.

- **Time to market:** Carrying out any change to the system in such cases becomes harder. In such environments, executing any business change takes time. This makes responding to market forces difficult--the business can also lose its market share. With the microservice architecture, we are addressing some of these challenges. This architecture provides greater flexibility and isolation for service deployment. It has proven to deliver much faster turnaround time and much needed business agility.

Understanding the deployment terminology

It is important that we understand the terminologies around microservices. This will help us navigate through much jargon and buzzwords. This sets our microservice journey on the right track:

- **Build**: In the build stage, the service source gets compiled without any errors along with the passing of all corresponding unit tests. This stage produces build artifacts.

- **Continuous Integration (CI)**: CI forces the entire application to build again every time a developer commits any change--the application code gets compiled and a comprehensive set of automated tests run against it. This practice emerged out of the problems of frequent integration of code in large teams. The basic idea is to keep the delta or change of the software small. This provides the required confidence of having software in a workable state. Even if a check-in made by a developer breaks the system, it is easy to fix it this way.

- **Deployment**: Hardware provisioning and installing the base OS and correct version of .NET framework installation are prerequisites to deployment. The next part of it is to promote these build artifacts in production through various stages. The combination of these two parts is referred to as the deployment stage. There is no distinction between the deployment and release stage in most monolithic applications.

- **Continuous Deployment (CD):** In CD practice, each successful build gets deployed to production. CD is more important from the technical team's perspective. Under CD, there are several other practices, such as automated unit testing, labeling and versioning of build number, and traceability of changes. With continuous delivery, the technical team ensures that the change pushed to production through various lower environments work as expected in production. Usually, these are smaller changes and deployed very quickly.

- **Continuous delivery:** Continuous delivery is different from CD. CD comes from the technical team's perspective, whereas continuous delivery is more focused toward giving the deployed code as early as possible to the customer. To make sure that customers get the right defect-free product, in continuous delivery, every build must pass through all the quality assurance checks. Once the product passes the satisfactory quality verification, it is the business stakeholders' decision when to release it.

- **Build and deployment pipelines**: Build and deployment pipeline is part of implementing continuous delivery through automation. It is a workflow of steps through which, code is committed in source repository. At the other end of the deployment pipeline, the artifacts for release are produced. Some of the steps that may be part of the build and deployment pipelines are as follows:
    1. Unit tests
    2. Integration tests
    3. Code coverage and static analysis
    4. Regression tests
    5. Deployments to staging environment
    6. Load/stress tests
    7. Deployment to release repository

- **Release**: A business feature made available to the end user is referred to as the release of a feature. To release a feature or service, the relevant build artifacts should be deployed beforehand. Usually, feature toggle manages the release of a feature. If the feature flag (also called feature toggle) is not switched on in production, it is called a dark release of the specified feature.

Prerequisites for successful microservice deployments

Any architectural style comes with a set of associated patterns and practices to follow. The microservice architectural style is no different. Microservice implementation has more chances of being successful with the adoption of the following practices:

- **Self-sufficient teams:** Amazon, who is a pioneer of SOA and microservice architectures, follows the *Two Pizza Teams* paradigm. This means usually a microservice team will have no more than 7-10 team members. These team members will have all the necessary skills and roles, for example, development, operations, and business analyst. Such a service team handles the development, operations, and management of a microservice.

- **CI and CD**: CI and CD are prerequisites for implementing microservices. Smaller self-sufficient teams, who can integrate their work frequently, are precursors to the success of microservices. This architecture is not as simple as monolith. However, automation and the ability to push code upgrades regularly enables teams to handle complexity. Tools, such as TFS, Team Foundation Online Services, Teamcity, and Jenkins, are quite popular toolchains in this space.

- **Infrastructure as code:** The idea of representing hardware and infrastructure components, such as networks with code, is new. It helps you make deployment environments, such as integration, testing, and production, look exactly identical. This means developers and test engineers will be able to easily reproduce production defects in lower environments. With tools such as CFEngine, Chef, Puppet, Ansible, and Powershell DSC, you can write your entire infrastructure as code. With this paradigm shift, you can also put your infrastructure under a version control system and ship it as an artifact in deployment.

- **Utilization of cloud computing:** Cloud computing is a big catalyst toward adopting microservices. It is not mandatory as such for microservice deployment, though. Cloud computing comes with near infinite scale, elasticity, and rapid provisioning capability. It is a no brainer that the cloud is a natural ally for microservices. So, knowledge and experience with the Azure cloud will help you adopt microservices.

Isolation requirements for microservice deployment

In 2012, Adam Wiggins, cofounder of the Heroku platform, presented 12 basic principles. These principles talk about defining new modern web applications from idea to deployment. This set of principles is now known as *12 factor App*. These principles paved the way for new architectural styles, which evolved into microservice architectures. One of the principles of 12 factor app was as follows:

> *"Execute the app as one or more stateless processes"*
> *- Adam Wiggins* (https://12factor.net/)

This means microservices are shared nothing architectures. So, services will be essentially stateless (except the database, which acts as the state store). The *shared nothing* principle is also applied across the entire spectrum of patterns and practices. This is nothing but isolation of components to achieve scale and agility.

In the microservice world, this principle of isolation is applied in the following ways:

- **Service teams**: There will be self-sufficient teams built around services. In effect, the teams will be able to take all the decisions necessary to develop and support the microservices they are responsible for.
- **Source control isolation:** The source repository of every microservice will be separate. It will not share any source code, files, and so on. It is okay to duplicate a few bits of code in the microservice world across services.
- **Build stage isolation**: Build and deploy pipelines for every microservice should be kept isolated. Build and deploy pipelines can even run in parallel, isolated, and deployed services. Due to this, CI-CD tools should be scaled to support different services and pipelines at a much faster speed.
- **Release stage isolation:** Every microservice should be released in isolation with other services. It is also possible that the same service with different versions is in the production environment.
- **Deploy stage isolation:** This is the most important part of isolation. Traditional monolith deployment is done with bare metal servers. With the advancement in virtualization, virtual servers have replaced bare metal servers.

In general, monoliths' standard release process looks like this:

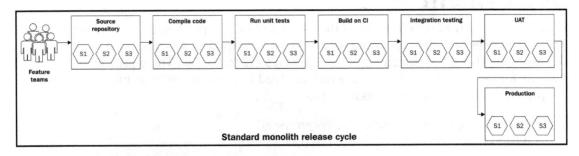

Considering these isolation levels, the microservice build and deployment pipeline may look like this:

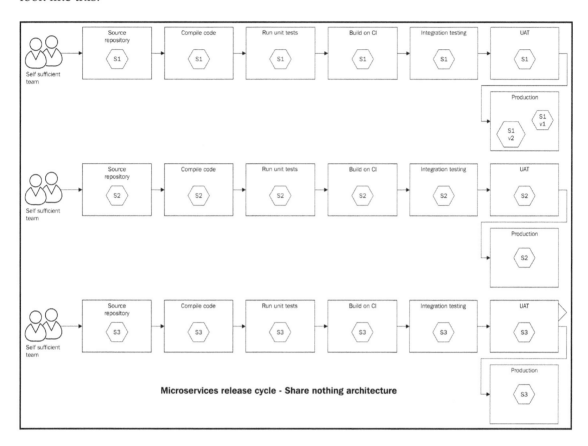

Microservices release cycle - Share nothing architecture

Need for a new deployment paradigm

The highest level of isolation for an application can be achieved by raising a new physical machine or bare metal server. So there is a server with its own operating system running on top of it and managing all system resources. This was regular stuff in legacy applications. But it is not practical for modern applications. Modern applications are massive systems. Some examples of these systems are Amazon, Netflix, and Nike, or even traditional financial banks, such as ING. These systems are hosted on tens of thousands of servers. These kinds of modern applications demand ultra-scalability to serve to their millions of users. For a microservice architecture, it does not make any sense to set up a new server just to run a small service on top of it.

With the new CPU architectural breakthroughs, one of the options that emerged is virtual machines. Virtual machines abstract out all the hardware interactions of an operating system through the hypervisor technology. Hypervisor enabled us to run many machines or servers on a single physical machine. One significant point to note is that all the virtual machines get their piece of isolated system resources from physical host resources.

This is still a good isolated environment to run the applications. Virtualization brought rationale to raise the server for the entire application. While doing so, it kept the components fairly isolated. This helped us utilize spare compute resources in our data centers. It improved the efficiency of our data centers while satisfying applications' fair isolation needs.

Yet, virtualization on its own is not able to support some of the microservice needs. Under the 12 factors principles, Adam also talks about this:

> *The twelve-factor app's processes are disposable, meaning they can be started or stopped at a moment's notice. This facilitates fast elastic scaling, rapid deployment of code or config changes, and robustness of production deploys.*
> *- Adam Wiggins* (https://12factor.net/)

This principle is important for the microservice architectural style. So, with microservices, ensure that the services spin faster. In this case, let's assume that there is one service per virtual machine. If we want to spin this service, it first needs to spin the virtual machine; however, the boot time of virtual machines is long. Another thing is that with such applications, we are talking about a lot of cluster deployments. So services will definitely be distributed in clusters. This also implies that virtual machines might need to be raised up on one of the nodes in the clusters and booted. This is again a problem with virtual machines' boot-up time. This does not bring the kind of efficiency that we are expecting for microservices.

Now, the only option left is to use the operating system process model, which comes with faster boot time. Processes' programming model has been well-known for ages. But even processes come at a cost. They are not well isolated and share system resources as well as the kernel of the operating system.

For microservices, we need a better isolation deployment model and a new paradigm of deployment. The answer is this: innovation of the container technology. A good consideration factor is that the container technology sits well between virtualization and the operating system's process model.

Containers

Container technology is not new to the Linux world. Containers are based on Linux's LXC technology. In this section, let's see how containers are important in the case of microservices.

What are containers?

A container is a piece of software in a complete filesystem. It contains everything that is needed to run: code, runtime, system tools, and system libraries--anything that can be installed on a server. This guarantees that the software will always run in the same way, regardless of its environment. Containers share their host operating system and kernel with other containers on the same host. The technology around containers is not new. It has been a part of the Linux ecosystem for a long time. Due to the recent microservice-based discussions around it, container technology came into the limelight again. Also, it is the technology on which Google, Amazon, and Netflix runs.

Suitability of containers over virtual machines

Let's understand the difference between containers and virtual machines--at the surface level, both are tools to achieve isolation and virtualization.

The architectural difference between virtual machines and containers is quite evident from the following diagram:

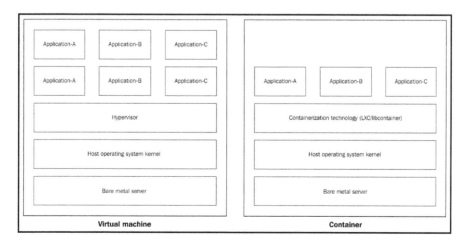

In virtual machine internals, we can see that there is a host operating system along with a kernel, and on top of it, the hypervisor layer. Hosted applications have to bring in their own operating system and environment. In containers though, the containerization technology layer serves as a single layer and is shared across different applications. This removes the need for a guest operating system. Thus, applications in a container come with a smaller footprint and strong isolation levels. Another aspect that will encourage you to use containers for microservice deployment is that we can pack more applications on the same physical machine when compared to the same applications deployed on a virtual machine. This helps us achieve greater economy of scale benefits and provides a comparison of the benefits of virtual machines.

One more thing to note with containers is that they can be run on virtual machines as well. So it is okay to have a physical server with a virtual machine on it. This virtual machine serves as a host to a number of containers.

Transformation of the operation team's mindset

Microsoft's Bill Baker came up with this analogy of pets and cattle and he applied it to the servers in the data center. Okay, honestly we care for our pets. We love them and show affection towards them, name them as well. We think of their hygiene; if they fall sick, we take them to the vet. Do we take such care of our cattle? Of course, we don't; this is because we do not care that much about cattle.

The same analogy is true with respect to servers and containers. In pre-DevOps days, server admins cared about servers. They used to name those server machines and also have dedicated maintenance downtime and so on. With DevOps practices, such as infrastructure as code and containerization, containers can be treated as cattle. As the operations team, we do not need to care for them since containers are meant for a short lifespan. They can be booted up quickly in clusters and teared down fast as well. When you are dealing with containers, always keep in mind this analogy. As far as daily operations go, expect the spinning up of and teardown of containers to act as normal.

This analogy itself changes the perspective towards microservice deployment and how it supports containerization.

Containers are new binaries

Containers are new binaries of deployment
- Steve Lasker, Principal Program Manager at Microsoft

This is a new reality you will face as a .NET developer: working with microservices. Containers are new binaries. With Visual Studio, we compile the .NET program. And after compilation, Visual Studio produces .NET assemblies, namely DLLs or EXE. We take this set of associated DLLs and EXEs emitted by the compiler and deploy them on the servers. So, in short, our deployment unit was in the form of assemblies. Not anymore! Well, we still have .the NET program generating EXEs and DLLs, but our deployment unit has changed in the microservice world. It is a container now. We will be still compiling programs into assemblies. These assemblies will be pushed to the container and ready to be shipped.

As you see the code walkthrough in the following section of this chapter, you will understand more about this point. We, as .NET developers, have the ability (and may I say necessity) to ship the containers. Along with this, another advantage of container deployment is that it removes the barrier between different operating systems and even different languages and runtimes.

It works on your machine? Let's ship your machine!

Usually, we hear this a lot from developers: *Well, it works on my machine!* This usually happens when there is a defect that is not reproducible in production. Since containers are immutable and composable, it is quite possible to eliminate the configuration impedance between the development and production environment.

Docker quick introduction

Docker (www.docker.com) is a company who has been a major force behind popularizing containerization of applications. Docker is to containers what Google is for search. Sometimes, people even use containers and Docker as synonyms. Microsoft has partnered with docker and is actively contributing to the docker platform and tools in open source. This makes docker important for us as .NET developers.

Docker is a very important topic and will be significant enough to learn for any serious .NET developer. However, due to time and scope constraints, we will just scratch the surface of the ecosystem of docker here. We strongly recommend that you read through the Docker books made available by Packt Publishing.

If you want to safely try and learn docker without even installing it on your machine, you can do so with https://KataCoda.com.

Now let's focus on some of the terminologies and tools of the Docker platform. This will be essential for our next section.

- **Docker image**: A Docker *image* is a read-only template with instructions for creating a Docker container. A Docker image consists of a separate filesystem and associated libraries and so on. Here, an image is always read-only and can run exactly the same abstracting underlying host differences. A Docker image can be composed as one layer on top of another. This composability of the Docker image can be compared with the analogy of layered cake. Docker images that are used across different containers can be reused. This also helps reduce the deployment footprint of applications that use the same base images.
- **Docker registry:** A Docker registry is a library of images. A registry can be either public or private. Also, it can be on the same server as the Docker daemon or Docker client or on a totally separate server.
- **Docker hub:** This is a public registry and it stores images. It is located at `http://hub.docker.com`.
- **Docker File**: Dockerfile is a build or scripting file that contains instructions to build a Docker image. There can be multiple steps documented in a Dockerfile, starting from getting the base image.
- **Docker container:** A Docker container is a runnable instance of a Docker image.
- **Docker compose:** Docker compose allows you to define an application's components--their containers, configuration, links, and volumes--in a single file. Then, a single command will set everything up and start your application. It is an architecture/dependency map for your application.
- **Docker swarm:** Swarm is the Docker service with which container nodes work together. It runs a defined number of instances of a replica task, which is itself a Docker image.

Let's look into the individual components of the Docker ecosystem; let's try to understand one of the ways in which the Docker workflow makes sense in the software development life cycle.

Microservice deployment with Docker overview

In order to support this workflow, we need a CI tool and a configuration management tool. For illustration purposes, we have taken the **Visual Studio Team Services** (**VSTS**) build service as CI and VSTS release management for continuous delivery. The workflow would remain the same for any other tools or modes of deployment. The following is one of the flavors of microservice deployment with Docker:

1. The code is checked into the Visual Studio team service repository. If this is the project's first check-in, it is done along with Dockerfile for the project.
2. The preceding check-in triggers VSTS to build the service from the source code and run unit/integration tests.
3. If tests are successful, VSTS builds a Docker image that is pushed to a *Docker registry*. VSTS release services deploy the image to the Azure container service.
4. If QA tests pass as well, VSTS is used to promote the container to deploy and start it in production.

The following diagram depicts the steps in detail:

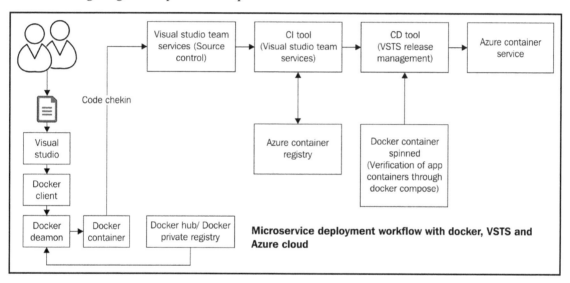

Microservice deployment workflow with docker, VSTS and Azure cloud

Note that usual .NET CI-CD tools, such as TeamCity and Octopus Deploy (capabilities are in alpha stage), have features to produce a Docker container as a build artifact and deploy it to production.

Microservice deployment example using Docker

Now we have all the essentials required to move toward coding and see for ourselves how things work. We have taken the product catalog service example here to be deployed as a Docker container. After running the source code accompanied, you should be able to successfully run the product catalog service in the Docker container.

We will follow the steps discussed next.

Setting up Docker on your machine

This tutorial doesn't require any existing knowledge of Docker and should take about 20 or 30 minutes to complete. Ready? Let's go!

Prerequisites

You will need to have the following software bits installed:

- Microsoft Visual Studio 2015 Update 3 (`https://www.visualstudio.com/downloads/download-visual-studio-vs`)
- .NET Core 1.0.1 - VS 2015 Tooling Preview 2 (`https://go.microsoft.com/fwlink/?LinkID=827546`)
- Docker For Windows to run your Docker containers locally (`https://www.docker.com/products/docker#/windows`)

Once Docker for Windows is installed, right-click on the Docker icon in the system tray and click on **Settings** and select **Shared Drives**:

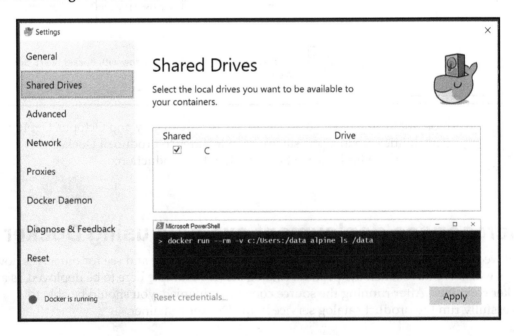

Creating an ASP.NET web application

Create a new project by navigating to **File** | **New Project** | **.NET Core** | Select **ASP.NET Core Web Application**, as per the following screenshot:

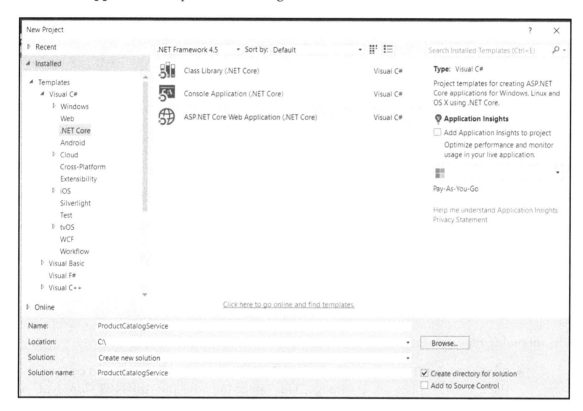

You can now delete `valuescontroller.cs` and `ProductCatalogService.cs` from the source code accompanied with this chapter.

Also, you can copy and replace the `launchSettings.json` file.

Adding Docker Support

Using Visual Studio, create a new ASP.NET Core Web application. When the application is loaded, either select **Add Docker Support** from the **PROJECT** menu or right-click on the project from the solution explorer and select **Add Docker Support** as shown in the following screenshot:

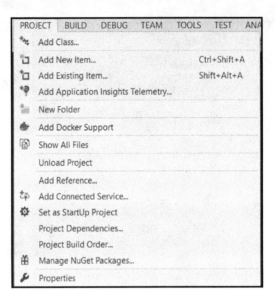

The following files are added to the project:

- `Dockerfile`: The `Docker` file for ASP.NET Core applications is based on the `microsoft/aspnetcore` image. This image includes the ASP.NET Core NuGet packages, which have been prejitted, improving startup performance. When building ASP.NET Core applications, the `Docker` file FROM instruction (command) points to the most recent `microsoft/dotnet` image on the Docker hub.
- `Docker-compose.yml`: This is the base `Docker-compose` file used to define the collection of images to be built and run with `Docker-compose` build/run.
- `Docker-compose.dev.debug.yml`: This is an additional `Docker-compose` file for iterative changes when your configuration is set to debug. Visual Studio will call `-f docker-compose.yml` and `-f docker-compose.dev.debug.yml` to merge them. This compose file is used by Visual Studio development tools.

- `Docker-compose.dev.release.yml`: This is an additional Docker Compose file to debug your release definition. It will load the debugger in isolation so it does not change the content of production image.

The `docker-compose.yml` file contains the name of the image that is created when the project is run.

The Dockerfile contents are straightforward:

```
FROM microsoft/aspnetcore:1.0.1
ENTRYPOINT ["dotnet", "ProductCatalogService.dll"]
ARG source=.
WORKDIR /app
EXPOSE 80
COPY $source .
```

Here's what each of these instructions does:

`FROM` tells Docker that to pull the base image on the existing image, call `microsoft/aspnetcore:1.0.1`. This image already contains all the dependencies for running the ASP.NET Core on Linux, so we don't have to set it.

`COPY` and `WORKDIR` copy the current directory's contents to a new directory inside the called/app container and set it to the working directory for subsequent instructions.

`EXPOSE` tells Docker to expose the product catalog service on port 80 of the container.

`ENTRYPOINT` specifies the command to execute when the container starts up. In this case, it's .NET.

Run and test the image in a live container. Now if you may have noticed in the last step, when you add Docker support to the **ProductCatalogService** project, Visual Studio adds **Docker** as an option in the run menu as well:

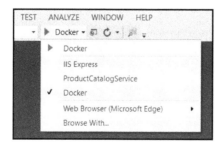

Now all you have to do is press *F5* and launch your service in the container. This is the easiest way to put your service in the container. Once your microservice is containerized, you can use Visual Studio team services and Azure container services to deploy your container to the Azure cloud.

Summary

Microservice deployment is an exciting journey for us. For successful microservice delivery, deployment best practices should be followed. We need to focus on implementing isolation requirements for microservices even before we talk about deployment using automated tools. With successful microservice deployment practices, we can deliver business changes rapidly. The different isolation requirements from self-sufficient teams to continuous delivery, give scale and agility that are fundamental promises of microservices. Containerization is by far one of the most important innovative technologies we have, and we must take advantage of it for microservice deployment. Combining Azure cloud with Docker will help us deliver the scale and isolation we are expecting from microservices. With Docker, we can easily achieve greater application density, which means reduction in our cloud infrastructure cost. We also saw how easy it is to start these deployments with Visual Studio and Docker tools for Windows.

In our next chapter, we will look at microservice security. We will discuss the Azure active directory for authentication, how to leverage OAuth 2.0, and how to secure an API gateway with Azure API Management.

6
Security

Security is one of the most important cross-cutting concerns for web applications. Unfortunately, data breaches of well-known sites seem common news these days. Taking this into account, information and application security has become critical to web applications. For the same reason, secure applications now should not be an afterthought. Security is everyone's responsibility in an organization.

Monolithic applications have less surface area when compared to microservices. However, microservices are distributed systems by nature. Also, in principle, microservices are isolated from each other. Hence, well-implemented microservices are more secure, compared to monolithic applications. Monolith has different attack vectors compared to microservices. The microservice architectural style forces us to think differently in the context of security. However, let me tell you upfront, microservice security is a complex domain to understand and implement.

Before we deep dive into microservice security, let's understand our approach toward it. We will be focusing more on how authentication and authorization (collectively referred to as *auth* in the chapter henceforth) work and the options available within the .NET ecosystem. We will explore Azure API management and its suitability as an API gateway for .NET-based microservice environments; we'll also see how Azure API management can help us protect microservices through its security features. Then, we'll briefly touch base with different peripheral aspects having *defense in depth* mechanisms for microservice security. We will also discuss the following topics along the line:

- Why form authentication and older techniques are not sufficient
- Authentication and the available options, including OpenID and Azure Active Directory
- Introducing OAuth 2.0
- Introducing Azure API management as an API gateway

- Using Azure API management for security
- Interservices communication security approaches
- Container security and other peripheral security aspects

Security in monolithic applications

To understand microservice security, let's step back and recall how we used to secure .NET monolithic applications. This will help us better grasp why a microservice's authentication and authorization mechanism needs to be different.

The critical mechanism to secure applications has always been authentication and authorization. Authentication verifies the *identity* of a user. Authorization manages what a user can or cannot access, which is nothing but *permissions*. And encryption, well, that's the mechanism that helps you protect data as it passes between the client and server. We're not going to discuss a lot about encryption, though. Just ensure the data that goes over the wire is encrypted everywhere. This is very well achieved through the use of the HTTPS protocol.

The following diagram depicts the flow of a typical authentication and authorization mechanism in .NET monoliths:

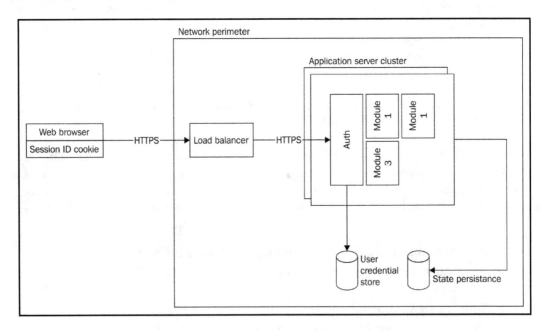

In the preceding diagram, we can see that the user enters his or her username and password typically through a **Web browser**. Then, this request hits some thin layer in a web application that is responsible for authentication and authorization. This layer or component connects to the user credential store, typically an SQL server in the case of a .NET application. The auth layer verifies user-supplied credentials against the username and password stored in the credential store.

Once the user credentials are verified for the session, a session cookie gets created on the browser. Unless the user has a valid session cookie, he cannot access the app. Typically, a session cookie is sent with every request. Within these kinds of monolithic applications, modules can freely interact with each other since they are in the same process and have in-memory access. This means trust is implicit within those application modules. So they do not need separate validation and verification of requests while talking to each other.

Security in microservices

Now let's look at the case of microservices. By nature, microservices are distributed systems. There is not a single instance of an application, rather, there are several distinct applications that coordinate with each other in harmony to produce the desired output.

Why traditional .NET auth mechanism won't work?

One of the possible approaches for microservice security might be this: we mimic the same behavior as that of the auth layer in a monolith. This could be depicted as follows:

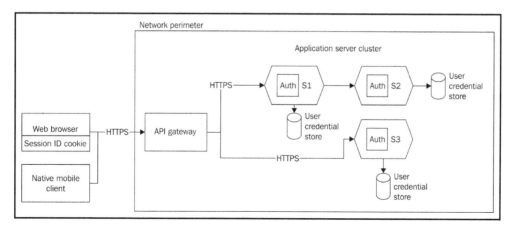

In this approach, we distributed the auth layer and provided it to all the microservices. Since each one is a different application, it will need its own auth mechanism. This inherently means that the user credential store is also different for every microservice. This raises so many questions, such as how do we keep the auth in sync across all services? How can we validate inter service communication or are we skipping it? We do not have satisfactory answers to these questions. Hence, this approach does not make sense and just increases complexity. With this approach, we can not even be sure whether it will work in the real world.

There is one more factor we need to take into account for modern applications. In the microservice world, we need to support native mobile apps, and other non-standard form factor devices as well as IoT applications. With the significant proliferation of native mobile applications, the microservice architecture also needs to support secure communication between those clients and microservices. This is different from the traditional web browser-based user interface. On mobile platforms, a web browser is not part of any native mobile app. This means cookie-based or session-based authentication is not possible. So microservices need to support this kind of interoperability between client applications. This was not at all a concern for .NET monolithic applications.

In the case of traditional authentication, the browser is responsible for sending the cookie upon each request. But we're not using the browser for a native mobile app. In fact, we're neither using ASPX pages, nor the form's authentication module. For an iOS client or Android, it's something different altogether. What's more, we are also trying to restrict unauthorized access to our API. In the preceding example, we'd be securing the client, be it an MVC app or a Windows phone app, and not the microservice. Moreover, all these mobile client devices are not part of the trust subsystem. For every request, we cannot trust that the mobile user is indeed the owner; the communication channel is not secured as well. So any request coming from them cannot be trusted at all.

But apart from these problems, there's another more conceptual problem we have. Why should the application be responsible for authenticating users and authorization? Shouldn't this be separated out?

One more solution to this is using the SAML protocol, but again, this is based on SOAP and XML, so not really a good fit for microservices. The complexity of the implementation of SAML is also high.

Therefore, it is evident from the preceding discussion that we need a token-based solution. The solution for microservices' auth comes in the form of OpenID Connect and OAuth 2.0. OpenID Connect is the standard for authentication and OAuth 2.0 is the specification for the authorization. However, this authorization is delegated by nature.

We will see this in detail in further sections. But before that, let's take a detour of JSON Web Token and see why they are significant with respect to microservice security.

JSON Web Tokens

JSON Web Tokens (JWT) is pronounced *JOT*. It is a well-defined JSON schema or format to describe the tokens involved in a data exchange process. JWTs are described in RFC 7519.

JWTs are not tied to either OpenID Connect or OAuth 2.0. This means they can be used independently, irrespective of OAuth 2.0 or OpenID Connect. OpenID Connect mandates the use of a JWT for all the tokens that are exchanged in the process. In OAuth 2.0, the use of JWTs isn't mandated but a kind of de facto implementation format. Moreover, the .NET framework has in-built support for JWT.

The purpose of a JWT-based security token is to produce a data structure that contains information about the issuer and the recipient along with a description of the sender's identity. Therefore, tokens should be protected over the wire so they could not be tampered with. To do so, tokens are signed with symmetric or asymmetric keys. This means when a receiver trusts the issuer of the token, it can also trust the information inside it.

Here is an example of a JWT:

```
eyJhbGciOiJIUzI1NiIsInR5cCI6IkpXVCJ9.eyJzdWIiOiIxMjM0NTY3ODkwIiwibmFtZSI6Ik
pvaG4gRG9lIiwiYWRtaW4iOnRydWV9.TJVA95OrM7E2cBab30RMHrHDcEfxjoYZgeFONFh7HgQ
```

This is the encoded form of a JWT. If we see the same token in decoded form, it has three components: header, payload, and signature; they are all separated by a period (.). The preceding example token can be decoded as follows:

Header: {"alg": "HS256", "type": "JWT"}

Payload: {"sub": "1234567890","name": "John Doe","admin": true}

Signature:HMACSHA256(base64UrlEncode(header) + "." + base64UrlEncode(payload),secret)

NET v.4.5.1 and onward has built-in support for generating and consuming JWTs. You can install JWT support in any .NET application using the package manager console and issuing the following command:

```
Install-Package System.IdentityModel.Tokens.Jwt
```

Via `https://jwt.io/`, you can view and decode JWTs very easily. Moreover, you can add it as part of Chrome debugger as well, which is quite handy.

What is OAuth 2.0?

Okay, you might not know what OAuth 2.0 is, but you surely have used it on several websites. Nowadays, many websites allow you to log in through your username and password with either Facebook, Twitter, or Google accounts. Land on your favorite website, for example, the `www.stackoverflow.com` login page. There is a login button that says you can sign in with your Google account, for example. When you click on the **Google** button, it takes you to Google's login page along with some permissions mentioned. Here you provide your Google username and password and click on the **Allow** button to grant permissions to your favorite site. Then Google redirects you to Stack Overflow and you are logged in with appropriate permissions in Stack Overflow. This is nothing but end user experience for OAuth 2.0 and OpenID Connect.

OAuth 2.0 can be best described as a series of specification turned authorization frameworks. RFC 6749 defines OAuth as follows:

> *The OAuth 2.0 authorization framework enables a third-party application to obtain limited access to an HTTP service, either on behalf of a resource owner by orchestrating an approval interaction between the resource owner and the HTTP service, or by allowing the third-party application to obtain access on its own behalf.*

OAuth 2.0 handles authorization in the Web, native mobile applications, and all headless server applications (these are nothing but microservice instances in our context). You must be wondering why we are discussing authorization first instead of authentication. The reason is that OAuth 2.0 is a delegated authorization framework. This means, to complete the authorization flow, it relies on an authentication mechanism.

Now let's see some terminologies associated with it.

OAuth 2.0 roles describes the involved parties in the authorization process:

1. **Resource**: The entity that is getting protected from unintended access and usage. This is nothing but a microservice in our case.
2. **Resource owner**: Resource owner is a person or entity who owns the specified resource. When a person owns a resource, he or she is an end user.

3. **Client**: Client is the term used to refer to all kinds of client applications. This refers to any application trying to access the protected resource. In microservices' context, the applications involved are single page application, web user interface client, and native mobile applications or even a microservice that is trying to access another microservice downstream.

4. **Authorization server**: This is the server that hosts the secure token service and issues tokens to the client after successfully authenticating the resource owner and obtaining permissions from the resource owner or their behalf.

You may have noticed that, OAuth does differentiate between end users and applications used by an end user. This is a bit odd but make perfect sense since it is also generally viewed as, *I am authorizing this app to perform these actions on my behalf.*

The following diagram depicts how these roles interact with each other in the general flow of authorization in the OAuth framework:

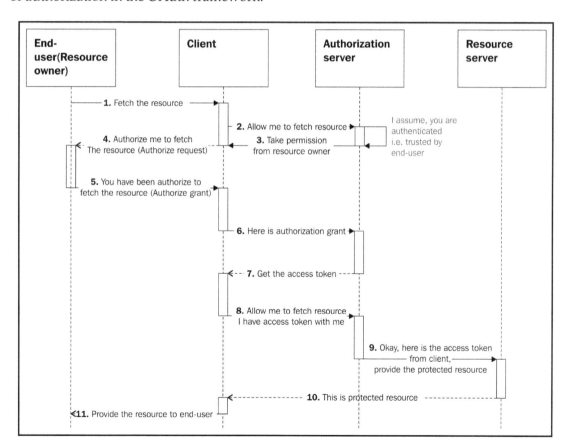

In step 6 illustrated in the preceding diagram, the client passes the authorization grant to the authorization server. This step is not as simple as it looks. Authorization grants are of different types. The grant types represent four different possible use cases for getting access tokens in oAuth 2.0. If you choose the wrong grant type, you might be compromising on security:

- **Authorization code**: This is the typical OAuth grant used by server-side web applications, the one you would use in your ASP.NET apps.
- **Implicit**: Authenticating with a server returns an access token to the browser, which can then be used to access resources. This is useful for single page applications where communication cannot be private.
- **Resource owner password credentials**: This requires the user to directly enter their username and password to the application. It is useful when you are developing a first-party application to authenticate with your own servers, for example, the mobile app might use a resource owner grant to authenticate with your own servers.
- **Client credentials**: This is typically used when the client is acting on its own behalf (the client is also the resource owner) or is requesting access to protected resources based on an authorization previously arranged with the authorization server.

What is OpenID Connect?

OpenID Connect 1.0 is a simple identity layer on top of the OAuth 2.0 protocol. OpenID Connect is all about authentication. It allows clients to verify end users based on the authentication performed by an authorization server. Also, it is used to obtain basic profile information about the end user in an interoperable and REST-like manner.

So OpenID Connect allows clients of all types--web-based, mobile, and JavaScript--to request and receive information about authenticated sessions and end users. We know that OAuth 2.0 defines access tokens. Well, OpenID Connect defines a standardized identity token (commonly referred to as ID token). The identity token is sent to the application so the application can validate who the user is. It defines an endpoint to get identity information for that user, such as their name or e-mail address. That's the user info endpoint.

It's built on top of OAuth 2.0, so the flows are the same. It can be used with the authorization code grant and implicit grant. It's not possible with the client credentials grant, as the client credentials grant is for server-to-server communication.

There's no end user involved in the process. So there's no end user identity either. Likewise, it doesn't make sense for the resource owner path of usage or process. Now how does that work? Well, instead of only requesting an access token, we'll request an additional ID token from the **security token service** (**STS**) that implements the OpenID Connect specification. The client receives an ID token, and usually, also an access token. To get more information for the authenticated user, the client can then send a request to the user info endpoint with the access token; this user info endpoint will then return the claims about the new user.

OpenID supports authorization code flow and implicit flow. It also adds some more additional protocols, which are discovery and dynamic registration.

Azure Active Directory

There are multiple providers for OAuth 2.0 and OpenID Connect 1.0 specifications. **Azure Active Directory** (**Azure AD**) is one of them. Azure AD provides organizations with enterprise-grade identity management for cloud applications. Azure AD integration will give your users a streamlined sign in experience, and it will help your application conform to the IT policy. Azure AD provides advanced security features, such as multifactor authentication, and scales really well with application growth. It is used in all Microsoft Azure Cloud products, including Office 365, and processes more than a billion sign ins per day.

One more interesting aspect of traditional .NET environments is that they can integrate their organizational windows server Active Directory with Azure AD really well. This can be done by Azure AD sync tool or the new capability of pass-through authentication. So, organizational IT compliances will still be managed.

Microservice Auth example with OpenID Connect, OAuth 2.0, and Azure AD

Now we are well-equipped with all the prerequisite knowledge to go for coding. Let's try and build a *ToDoList* application. We are going to secure TodoListService, which represents one of our microservices. In the solution, the ToDoList microservice is represented by the TodoListService project. And *ToDoListWebApp* represents the server-side web application. It will be easier to follow if you open up the Visual Studio solution named `OpenIdOAuthAzureAD.sln` provided with this chapter. This example uses the client credentials grant.

Note that due to the ever-changing nature of Azure portal and the corresponding Azure services UI, it is advisable that you use the Azure Service management API and automate some of the registration tasks about to follow. However, for understanding purposes and largely for encouraging developers who are new to Azure or might be trying Azure AD for the first time, we are going to follow the Azure portal user interface.

Here are the prerequisites:

- Visual Studio 2013 with update 3 or Visual Studio 2015
- An Azure subscription (if you don't have this, you can use the free trial account for this demo)
- Azure AD tenant (single-tenant): You can also work with your Azure account's own default directory, which should be different from that of the Microsoft organization.

Step 1 – Registration of TodoListService and TodoListWebApp with Azure AD tenant

Now let's look at how to register TodoListService.

In this step, we will add TodoListService with Azure AD tenant. To achieve this, log in to the Azure management portal, then do this:

1. Click on **App registrations**. Click on **Add** button. It will open the **Create** pane, as depicted here:

2. Provide all the mandatory details as displayed in the preceding diagram and click on the **create** button at the bottom of the **Create** pane. While we are providing a sign-on URL, make sure that you are providing it for your app. In our case, TodoListService is a microservice, so we won't have a special sign-in URL. Hence, we have to provide the default URL or just the hostname of our microservice. Here we are going to run the service from our machine, so the localhost URL will be sufficient. You can find the sign-in URL once you right-click on project URL under `TodoListService` project|**Web**, as shown in the following diagram:

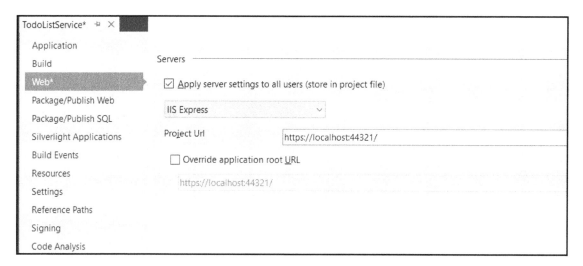

A sign-in URL in Azure portal should have the trailing `/`; otherwise, you may face an error, even if you execute all the steps correctly.

3. If you deploy your service with the Microsoft Azure App Service plan, you will get a URL that is similar to `https://todolistservice-xyz.azurewebsites.net /`. You can later change the sign-on URL if you deploy the service on Azure.

4. Once you click on the **Create** button, Azure will add the application to your Azure AD Tenant. However, there are still a few more details that need to be completed for finishing the registration of TodoListService. So navigate to **App Registration** | **TodoListService** | **Properties**. You will notice that there are a few more additional properties, such as App ID URI, which has been provided now.

5. For the App ID URI, enter `https://[Your_Tenant_Name]/TodoListService`, replacing `[Your_Tenant_Name]` with the name of your Azure AD tenant. Click on **OK** to complete the registration. The final configuration should look like this:

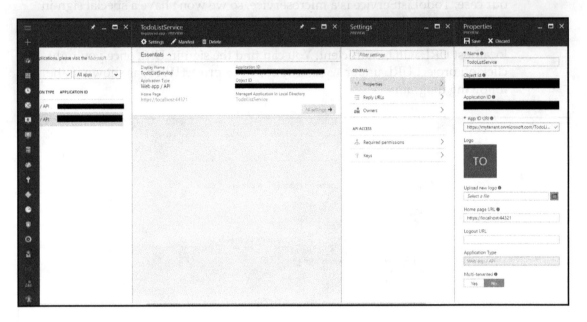

Now we move on to the registration of **TodoListWebApp**.

- First, we register TodoListWebApp. This is necessary since we are going to use OpenID Connect to connect to this browser-based web application. So we need to establish the trust between the end user, that is, us and TodoListWebApp.
- Click on **App registrations**. Click on the **Add** button. It will open up the **Create** pane, as depicted in the following screenshot. Fill in the sign-in URL as `https://localhost:44322/`.

- Once again, as in the TodoListService registration, we will be able to view most of the additional properties once we create the web app. So, the final properties configuration will look like this:

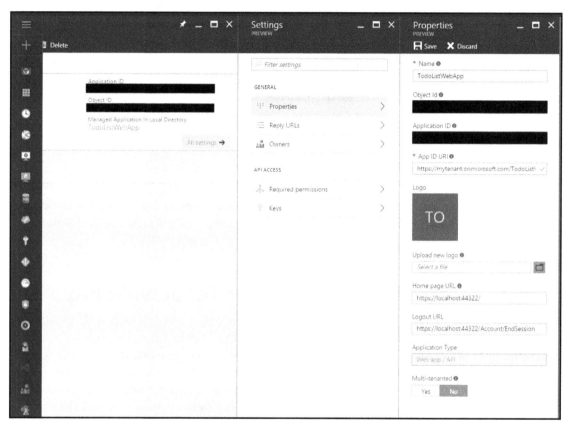

- A setting to note here is the logout URL: we set it as `https://localhost`
  `:44322/Account/EndSession`.

  This is because after ending the session, Azure AD will redirect the user to this URL. For the App ID URI, enter `https://[Your_AD_Tenant_Name]/TodoListWeb`
  `App`, replacing `[Your_AD_Tenant_Name]` with the name of your Azure AD tenant. Click on **OK** to complete the registration.

- Now we need to set up permissions between **TodoListWebApp** so that it can call our microservice: TodoListService. So, navigate to **App Registration** | **TodoListWebApp** | **Required Permissions** again and click on **Add**. Now click on **1 Select an API**. This navigation is displayed in the following screenshot. You need to key in ToDoListService for it to show up in the API pane.

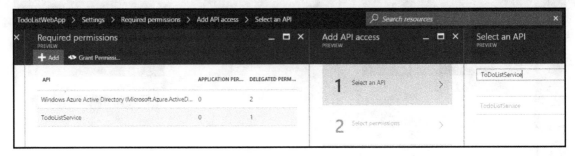

- Now you will be able to view the **Enable Access** pane, where you have to tick for Access **TodoListService** permissions under delegated permissions and done under the **Add API access** pane. This will save the permissions.

Step 2 – Generation of AppKey for TodoListWebApp

Another important step for registration is putting `client_secret`, which is necessary to establish trust between Azure AD and TodoListWebApp. This `client_secret` is generated only once and configured in the web application. To generate this key, navigate to **App Registrations** | **TodoListWebApp** | **Keys**. Then, add the description as `AppKey` and click on **save**. Once the key is saved, the value of the key is autogenerated by Azure and will be displayed next to the description. This key is displayed only once, so you have to immediately copy it and save it for later purposes. We will be keeping this key in the `web.config` file of TodoListWebApp in this case.

The key stored will be displayed on the Azure portal as follows:

 For production-grade applications, it is a bad idea to keep `client_Secret` and all such critical key values in `web.config`. It is good practice to keep them encrypted and isolated from applications. For such purposes, in production-grade applications, you can use Azure key-vault (`https://azure.microsoft.com/en-us/services/key-vault/`) to keep all your keys protected. Another advantage of key vault is that you can manage the keys according to the environment, such as dev-test-staging and production.

Step 3 – Configuring Visual Studio solution projects

First we look at how to configure this with the **TodoListService** project.

Open the `web.config` file and replace the following keys:

1. Search for the `ida:Tenant` key. Replace its value with your AD tenant name, for example, `contoso.onmicrosoft.com`. This will also be part of any of the application's APP ID URI.
2. Replace the `ida:Audience` key. Replace its value with `https://[Your_AD_Tenant_Name]/TodoListService`. Replace `[Your_AD_Tenant_Name]` with the name of your Azure AD tenant.

Now let's see how to configure this with the **TodoListWebApp** project.

Open the `web.config` file and find and replace the following keys with the provided values:

1. Replace `todo:TodoListResourceid` with `https://[Your_Tenant_Name]/TodoListService`.

2. Replace `todo:TodoListBaseAddress` with `https://localhost:44321/`.

3. Replace `ida:ClientId` with the application ID of **ToDoListWebApp**. You can get it by navigating to **App Registration | TodoListWebApp**.

4. Replace `ida:AppKey` with `client_secret` that we generated in step 2 of the process of registering **TodoListWebApp**. If you missed noting this key, you need to delete the previous key and regenerate a new key again.

5. Replace `ida:Tenant` with your AD tenant name, for example, `contoso.onmicrosoft.com`.

6. Replace `ida:RedirectUri` with the URL you want the application to redirect to when the user signs out of TodoListWebApp. In our case, the default is `https://localhost:44322/` since we want the user to navigate to the home page of the application.

Step 4 – Generate client certificates on IIS Express

Now TodoListService and TodoListWebApp will talk over a secure channel. To establish a secure channel, ToDoListWebApp needs to trust the client certificate. Both services are hosted on the same machine and run on IIS Express.

To configure your computer to trust the IIS Express SSL certificate, open the PowerShell command window as the administrator. Query your personal certificate store to find the thumbprint of the certificate for `CN=localhost`:

```
PS C:windowssystem32> dir Cert:LocalMachineMy
Directory: Microsoft.PowerShell.SecurityCertificate::LocalMachineMy
Thumbprint                              Subject
----------                              -------
C24798908DA71693C1053F42A462327543B38042  CN=localhost
```

Next, add the certificate to the Trusted Root store:

```
PS C:windowssystem32> $cert = (get-item
cert:LocalMachineMyC24798908DA71693C1053F42A462327543B38042)
PS C:windowssystem32> $store = (get-item cert:LocalmachineRoot)
PS C:windowssystem32> $store.Open("ReadWrite")
PS C:windowssystem32> $store.Add($cert)
PS C:windowssystem32> $store.Close()
```

The preceding set of instructions will add a client certificate to the local machine's certificate store.

Step 5 – Run both the applications

We are done with all those tedious configuration screens and replacing of keys. Excited? But before you hit *F5*, set ToDoListService and ToDoListWebApp as startup projects. Once this is done, we can safely run our application and be greeted with the landing page of our application. If you click on the **sign-in** button, you will be redirected to `login.microsoftonline.com`; this represents the Azure AD login. Once you are able to log in, you will see the landing page as follows:

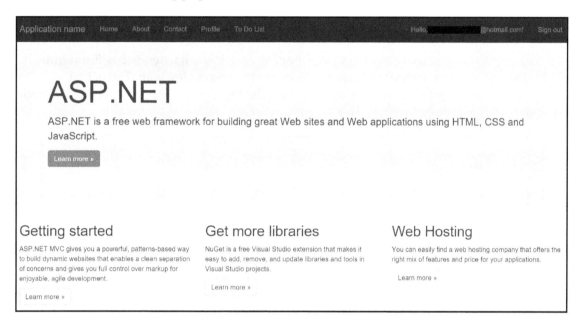

You can observe network traffic and URL redirection when you log in to the application to study a detailed exchange of ID tokens and get an access token. If you explore the application through the To Do List menu, you will be able to access the To Do List screen as well as add items to To Do List. This is where our TodoListService microservice is getting called as well as getting authorization permissions from the TodoWebApp web application. If you explore the profile menu, you will see the ID token return along with your first name, last name, and e-mail ID, which shows OpenID Connect in action.

If you want to explore the code in detail, `TodoListController.cs` in **TodoListService** project, `Startup.Auth.cs`, and `TodoListController.cs` contains interesting bits of code along with explanatory comments.

In this example, we used OAuth and OpenID Connect to secure a browser-based user interface, a web application, and a microservice. Things might be different if we have an API gateway between the user interface web app and microservice. In this case, we need to establish trust between the web app and API gateway. Also, we have to pass the ID token and access token from the web app to the API gateway. This, in turn, passes the tokens to the microservice. However, it is not feasible to cover the discussion and implementation in this chapter's scope.

Azure API management as an API gateway

Another important pattern in microservices' implementation is **Backends For Frontends (BFF)**. This pattern was introduced and made popular by Sam Newman. The actual implementation of the BFF pattern is done by introducing the API gateway between various types of clients and microservices. This is depicted in the following diagram:

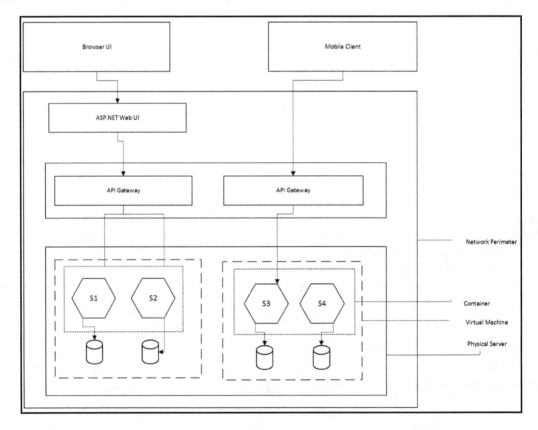

Azure API Management (henceforth referred to as Azure APIM or just APIM) is just the right fit, and it can act as an API gateway in .NET-based microservice implementation. Since Azure APIM is one of the cloud services, it is ultra-scalable and can be integrated well within the Azure ecosystem. In the current chapter, we will focus on the following features of Azure APIM.

Azure APIM is logically divided into three parts:

- **API gateway**: API Gateway is nothing but a proxy between client applications and services. It is responsible for the following functionalities; this is mainly used by various applications to talk to microservices:
    - Accepts API calls and routes them to your backends
    - Verifies API keys, JWTs, and certificates
    - Supports auth through Azure AD and OAuth 2.0 access token
    - Enforces usage quotas and rate limits
    - Transforms your API on the fly without code modifications
    - Caches backend responses where set up
    - Logs call metadata for analytics purposes
- **Publisher portal**: This is the administrative interface to organize and publish an API program. It is mainly used by microservice developers to make microservices/APIs available to API consumers or client applications. Through this, API developers can:
    - Define or import API schema
    - Package APIs into products
    - Set up policies such as quotas or transformations on the APIs
    - Get insights from analytics
    - Manage users
- **Developer portal**: This serves as the main web presence for API consumers where they can do this:
    - Read the API documentation
    - Try out an API via the interactive console
    - Create an account and subscribe to it to get the API keys
    - Access analytics on their own usage

Azure APIM comes with an easy-to-follow user interface and good documentation. Azure API management also comes with its REST API, hence all the capabilities of the Azure APIM portal, which you see can see, can be programmatically achieved by Azure REST API endpoint available for Azure APIM.

Now, let's quickly look at some security-related concepts in Azure APIM and how they can be used in microservices:

 1. Products: Products are nothing but a collection of APIs. They also contain usage quota and terms of use.

2. Policies: Policies is one of the dynamic security features of API management. They allow the publisher to change the behavior of the API through configuration. Policies are a collection of statements that are executed sequentially upon the request or response of an API. API management is fundamentally a proxy that is sitting between our microservices hosted in Azure and client applications. By virtue of the fact that it is an intermediate layer, it is able to provide additional services. These additional services are defined in a declarative XML-based syntax called policies. Azure APIM allows various policies. In fact, you can compose your own custom policies by combining the existing ones. A few of the important policies are mentioned next.

- **Access restriction policies:**
  - Check the HTTP header: This policy checks whether a specific HTTP header or its value exists in every request received by Azure APIM.
  - Limit call rate by subscription: This policy provides allow or deny access to the microservice based on the number of times the specific service has been called on a per subscription basis.
  - Restrict caller IPs: This policy refers to whiteboxing of IP addresses so only known IPs can access the services.
  - Set usage quota by subscription: This policy allows a number of calls. It allows you to enforce a renewable or lifetime call volume and/or bandwidth quota on a per subscription basis.
  - Validate JWT: This policy validates the JWT token parameter that is used for auth in applications.

- **Authentication policies:**
    - Authenticate with basic : This policy helps apply basic authentication over the incoming request.
    - Authenticate with client certificate: This policy helps carry out authentication of a service that is behind the API gateway, using client certificates.

- **Cross domain policies**
    - Allow cross-domain calls: This policy enables us to make CORS requests through Azure APIM.
    - CORS : This adds CORS support to an endpoint or a microservice to allow cross-domain calls from browser-based web applications.
    - JSONP: The JSONP policy adds JSON padding (JSONP) support to an endpoint or entire microservice to allow cross-domain calls from Java Script web applications.

- **Transformation policies**
    - Mask URLs in content: This policy masks URLs in response; it does so via Azure APIM.
    - Set backend service: This policy alters the behavior of the backend service of an incoming request.

Another great thing about policies is they can be applied for inbound and outbound requests.

3. Rate limit and quota policy example:

As in preceding section, we have seen what is meant by policy. Now let's see an example. The following is one of the quota policies applied for an endpoint:

```
<policies>
<inbound>
    <!-- Change the quota to immediately see the effect-->
    <rate-limit calls="100" renewal-period="60">
    </rate-limit>
    <quota calls="200" renewal-period="604800">
    </quota>
    <base />
</inbound>
<outbound>
  <base/>
  </outbound>
</policies>
```

In this example, we are limiting incoming requests (inbound) from a single user. So, an API user can only make 100 calls within 60 seconds. If they try to make more calls within that duration, the user will get an error with status code 429, which basically states *Rate limit is exceeded*. Also, we are assigning the quota limit of 200 calls in a year for the same user. This kind of throttling behavior is a great way to protect microservices from unwanted requests and even DOS attacks.

Azure APIM also supports Auth with OAuth 2.0 and OpenID Connect. Inside the publisher portal, you can easily see OAuth and OpenID Connect tabs to configure the providers.

Container security

Docker is a grand force around containerization of applications in the industry. With widespread usage of containers, it is evident that we need to have effective security measures around containers. If we take a look at the internal architecture of containers, they are quite close to the host operating system kernel.

Docker applies the principle of least privilege to provide isolation and reduce the attack surface. Despite the advances, the following points will help you understand the security measures you can take around containers:

- Ensure all the container images used for microservices are signed and originate from a trusted registry
- Harden the host environment, the daemon process, and images
- Follow the principle of least privilege and do not elevate access to access devices
- Use control groups in Linux to manage keeping a tab on resources, such as memory, I/O, and CPU
- Even though containers live for a very short duration, logging all of the container activity is advisable and important to understand for post analysis
- If possible, integrate the container scanning process with tools, such as aqua (`http://www.aquasec.com`) or Twistlock (`https://www.twistlock.com`)

Other security best practices

The microservice architectural style is new, although some of the security practices around the infrastructure and writing secure code are still applicable. In this section, let's discuss some of these practices:

- **Standardization of libraries and frameworks:** There should be a process to introduce new libraries and frameworks or tools in the development process. This will ease out patching in case any vulnerability is found; it will also minimize the risks introduced by ad hoc implementation of libraries or tools around development.

- **Regular vulnerability identification and mitigation**: Using the industry standard vulnerability scanner to scan the source code and binaries should be a regular part of development. The findings and observations should be addressed as equally as functional defects.

- **Third-party audits and pen testing:** External audits and penetration testing exercises are immensely valuable. There should be a regular practice of conducting such exercises. This is quite essential in applications where mission critical or sensitive data is handled.

- **Logging and monitoring**: Logging is quite a useful technique for detecting and recovering from attacks. Having the capability of aggregating logs from different systems is essential in the case of microservices. Tools such as riverbed, AppDynamics, and Splunk are quite useful in this space.

- **Firewalls**: Having one or more firewall at network boundaries is always beneficial. Firewall rules should be properly configured.

- **Network segregation**: Network partitioning is constrained and limited in the case of monoliths. However, with microservices, we need to logically create different network segments and subnets. Segmentation based on microservices' interaction patterns can be very effective to keep and develop additional security measures.

Summary

The microservice architectural style being distributed by design gives us better options to protect valuable business critical system. Traditional .NET-based authentication and authorization techniques are not sufficient and cannot be applied to the microservice world. We also saw why secure-token-based approaches, such as OAuth 2.0 and OpenID Connect 1.0, are becoming de facto standards for microservice authorization and authentication. If you want to have more general information related to security, do visit **Open Web Application Security Project (OWASP)** at `http://www.owasp.org` and Microsoft Security development life cycle at `https://www.microsoft.com/en-us/sdl/`. Azure AD can very well support OAuth 2.0 and OpenID Connect 1.0. Azure API Management can also act as an API gateway in microservices' implementation and also provide nifty security features, such as policies.

Azure AD and Azure API management provide quite a few powerful capabilities to monitor and log the requests received. This will be quite useful, not only for security but also for tracing and troubleshooting scenarios. We will see logging, monitoring, and the overall instrumentation around troubleshooting of microservices in the next chapter.

7
Monitoring

When something goes wrong in a system, the concerned stakeholders will want to know what has happened, why it has happened and any hint or clue for fixing it, and how to prevent the same problem from occurring again in the future. This is one of the primary uses of monitoring. However, monitoring spans well beyond this primary usage.

In .NET monoliths, there are multiple monitoring solutions available to choose from. Also, the monitoring target is always centralized, and monitoring is certainly easy to set up and configure. If something breaks down, we know what to look for and where to look for it since only a finite number of components participate in a system, and they have a fairly long life span.

However, microservices are distributed systems and, by nature, more complex than monoliths. So resource utilization and health and performance monitoring are quite essential in a microservice production environment. We can use this diagnostic piece of information to detect and correct issues and also to spot potential problems and prevent them from occurring. Monitoring microservices presents different challenges. In this chapter, we will primarily discuss the following topics:

- The need for monitoring
- Monitoring and logging challenges in microservices
- Available tools and strategies for microservices in the .NET monitoring space
- Use of Azure diagnostics and application insight
- A brief overview of the ELK stack and Splunk

What does monitoring really mean? There is no formal definition of monitoring; however, the following is appropriate:

> *Monitoring provides information around the behavior of an entire system or different parts of a system in their operational environment. This information can be used for diagnosing and gaining insight into the different characteristics of a system.*

Instrumentation and telemetry

A monitoring solution is dependent upon instrumentation and telemetry. So it is natural that when we speak about monitoring microservices, we also discuss instrumentation and telemetry data. Logs are nothing but an instrumentation mechanism.

Instrumentation

Now let's see what is instrumentation. Instrumentation is one of the ways through which you can add diagnostic features to applications. It can be formally defined like this:

> *Most applications will include diagnostic features that generate custom monitoring and debugging information, especially when an error occurs. This is referred to as instrumentation and is usually implemented by adding event and error handling code to the application. -MSDN*

Under normal conditions, data from some informational events may not be required, thus reducing the cost of storage and the transactions required to collect it. However, when there is an issue with the application, you have to update the application configuration so that the diagnostic and instrumentation systems can collect informational event data as well as error and warning messages to assist in isolating and fixing faults. It may be necessary to run the application in this extended reporting mode for some time if the problem appears only intermittently.

Telemetry

Telemetry, in its most basic form, is the process of gathering information generated by instrumentation and logging systems. Typically, it is performed using asynchronous mechanisms that support massive scaling and wide distribution of application services. It can be defined as follows:

> *The process of gathering remote information that is collected by instrumentation is usually referred to as telemetry. -MSDN*

In large and complex applications, information is usually captured in a data pipeline and stored in a form that makes it easier to analyze and capable of presenting information at different levels of granularity. This information is used to discover trends, gain insight into usage and performance, and detect and isolate faults.

Azure has no built-in system that directly provides a telemetry and reporting system of this type. However, a combination of the features exposed by all the Azure services, Azure diagnostics, and application insight allows you to create telemetry mechanisms that span the range of simple monitoring mechanisms to comprehensive dashboards. The complexity of the telemetry mechanism you require usually depends on the size of the application. This is based on several factors, such as the number of roles or virtual machine instances, the number of ancillary services it uses, the distribution of the application across different data centers, and other related factors.

The need for monitoring

Microservices are complex, distributed systems. Microservice implementation is the backbone of any modern IT business. Understanding the internals of the services along with their interactions and behaviors will help you make the overall business more flexible and agile. The performance, availability, scale, and security of microservices can directly affect a business and also its revenue. Hence, monitoring microservices is vital. It helps us observe and manage the quality of the service attributes. Let's discuss the scenarios where it is required.

Health monitoring

With health monitoring, we monitor the health of a system and its various components at a certain frequency, typically a few seconds. This ensures that the system and its components behave as expected. With the help of an exhaustive health monitoring system, we can keep tabs on the overall system health, which has data points, such as CPU, memory utilization, and so on. It might be in the form of pings or extensive health monitoring endpoints, which emit the health status of services along with some useful metadata at that point in time.

For health monitoring, we can use the rate of request failures and successes; we can also utilize techniques such as synthetic user monitoring. We will see synthetic user monitoring a little later in this chapter.

The metrics for heath monitoring are based on the threshold values of success or failure rates. If the parameter value goes out of the configured threshold, an alert is triggered. It is quite possible that some preventive action to maintain the health of the system would be triggered due to this failure. This action can be something like restarting the service in the failure state or provisioning some server resource.

Availability monitoring

Availability monitoring is quite similar to health status monitoring, which we just discussed. However, the subtle difference is that in availability monitoring, the focus is on the availability of systems rather than a snapshot of the health at that point in time.

Availability of systems is dependent on various factors, such as the overall nature and domain of the application, services, and service dependencies as well as infrastructure or environment. The availability monitoring system captures low-level data points related to these factors and represents them so as to make a business-level feature available. Many times, availability monitoring parameters are used to track business metrics and **service level agreements (SLA)**.

Performance monitoring

The performance of a system is often measured by key performance indicators. Some of the key performance indicators of any large web-based system are as follows:

- The number of requests served per hour
- The number of concurrent users served per hour
- The average processing time required by users to perform business transactions, for example, placing an order

Additionally, performance is also gauged by system-level parameters, such as:

- CPU utilization
- Memory utilization
- I/O rates
- Number of queued messages

If any of these key performance indicators is not met by the system, an alert is raised.

Often, while analyzing performance issues, historical data from previous benchmarks - captured by the monitoring system , is used to troubleshoot.

Security monitoring

Monitoring systems can detect unusual data pattern requests or even unusual resource consumption patterns and detect attacks on the system. Specifically, in the case of DOS, attacks or injection attacks could be identified beforehand and the teams could be alerted. Security monitoring also keeps audit trails of authenticated users and gives a history of the users who have checked in and out of the system. It also comes in handy for getting satisfying compliance requirements.

Security is a cross-cutting aspect of distributed systems, including microservices. So there are multiple avenues of getting such data generated in the system. Security monitoring can get data from various tools that are not part of the system but may be part of the infrastructure or environment in which the system is hosted. Different types of logs and database entries can serve as data sources. However, this really depends upon the nature of the system.

SLA monitoring

Systems with SLAs basically guarantee certain characteristics, such as performance and availability. For cloud-based services, this is a pretty common scenario. Essentially, SLA monitoring is all about monitoring those guaranteed SLAs for the system. SLA monitoring is enforced as a contractual obligation between a service provider and consumer.

It is often defined on the basis of availability, response time, and throughput. Data points required for SLA monitoring can come from performance endpoint monitoring or logging and availability of monitoring parameters. For internal applications, many organizations track the number of incidences raised due to service downtime. The action taken against these incidences' **Root Cause Analysis** (**RCA**) mitigates the risk of repeating those issues and helps meet the SLAs.

For internal purposes, an organization might also track the number and nature of incidents that had caused the service to fail. Learning how to resolve these issues quickly or eliminate them completely helps reduce downtime and meet SLAs.

Auditing sensitive data and critical business transactions

For any legal obligations or compliance reasons, the system might need to keep audit trails of user activities in the system and record all their data accesses and modifications. Since audit information is highly sensitive in nature, it might be disclosed only to a few privileged and trusted individuals in the system. Audit trails can be part of a security subsystem or separately logged. You may need to transfer and store audit trails in a specific format, as stated by the regulation or compliance specifications.

End user monitoring

In end user monitoring, the usage of the features of the system and/or the overall system usage by the end users is tracked and logged. Usage monitoring could be done using various user-tracking parameters, such as the features used, the time required to complete a critical transaction for the specified user, or even enforced quotas. (Enforced quotas are constraints or limits put on an end user in regard to system usage. In general, various pay-as-you-go services use enforced quotas, for example, a free trial, where you can upload files only up to 25 MB.) The data source for this type of monitoring is typically collected in terms of logs and tracking user behavior.

Troubleshooting system failures

The end users of a system might experience system failures. This can be in the form of either a system failure or a situation where users are not able to perform a certain activity. These kinds of issues are monitored using system logs; if not, the end user would need to provide a detailed information report. Also, sometimes server crash dumps or memory dumps can be immensely helpful. However, in the case of distributed systems, it will be a bit difficult to understand the exact root cause of the failures.

In many scenarios of monitoring, using only one monitoring technique is not effective. It is better to use multiple monitoring techniques and tools for diagnostics. In particular monitoring a distributed system is quite challenging and requires data from various sources. In addition to analyzing the situation properly and deciding on the action points, we must consider a holistic view of monitoring rather than looking into only one type of system perspective.

Now that we have a better idea about what needs to be done for general purpose monitoring, let's revisit the microservice perspective. So we will discuss the different monitoring challenges presented by the microservice architectural style.

Monitoring challenges

Microservice monitoring presents different challenges. Let's check them out first in this section:

- **Scale**: One service could be dependent upon the functionality provided by various other microservices. This yields complexity, which is not usual in the case of .NET monolith systems. Instrumenting all these dependencies is quite difficult. Another problem that comes along with scale is the rate of change. With the advancement of continuous deployment and container-based microservices, the code is always in a deployable state. Containers always live for minutes, if not seconds. The same is true for virtual machines. Virtual machines have a life of around a couple of minutes to a couple of hours. In such a case, measuring regular signals, such as CPU usage and memory consumption usage per minute, does not make sense. Container instances sometimes might not be alive for a minute. Before a minute passes, the container instance might have been disposed. This is one of the challenges of microservice monitoring.

- **DevOps mindset**: Traditionally, services or systems once deployed are owned and cared for by the operational teams. However, DevOps promises to break down the silos between developers and operations teams. It comes with lots of practices, such as continuous integration and continuous delivery as well as continuous monitoring.

    Along with these new practices come new toolsets.

    However, DevOps is not just a set of practices or tools; it is, more importantly, a mindset. It is always a difficult and slow process to change the mindset of people. Microservice monitoring also requires a similar mindset shift.

    With the emergence of autonomy of services, developer teams now have to own services. This also means that they have to work through and fix development issues as well as keep an eye on all operational parameters and SLAs of the services. Just by using state-of-the-art monitoring tools, development teams will not be transformed overnight. This is true for operational teams as well. It won't suddenly become a *core platform team* (or whatever fancy name you prefer) overnight.

    To make microservices successful and meaningful for organizations, developers and operations teams need to help each other understand their own pain points and also think in the same direction, that is, how they can deliver value to the business together. Monitoring cannot happen without the instrumentation of services, which is the part where developer teams can help. And, alerting and setting up of operational metrics and running books won't happen without the operational team's help. This is one of the challenges in delivering microservice monitoring solutions.

- **Data flow visualization:** There are a number of tools present on the market for data flow visualization. Some of them are AppDynamics, New Relic, and so on. These tools are capable of handling visualization of 10 to, maybe, 100s of microservices. However, in larger settings, where there are thousands of microservices, these tools are unable to handle visualization. This is one of the challenges in microservice monitoring.

- **Testing of monitoring tools**: We trust monitoring tools with the understanding that they depict a factual representation of the big picture of our microservice implementation. However, to make sure that they remain true to this understanding, we will have to test the monitoring tools. This is never a challenge in monolith implementations. However, when it comes to microservices, visualization of microservices is required for monitoring purposes. This means generating fake/synthetic transactions and time and utilizing the entire infrastructure rather than serving the customer. Hence, the testing of monitoring tools is a costly affair and presents a significant challenge in microservice monitoring.

Monitoring strategies

In this section, we will take a look at the monitoring strategies that will make microservices observable. It is common to implement the following or more strategies to create a well-defined and holistic monitoring solution:

- **Application/system monitoring:** This strategy is also called a framework-based strategy. Here, the application, or in our case microservice, itself generates the monitoring information within the given context of execution. The application can be dynamically configured based on the thresholds or trigger points in the application data, which can generate tracing statements. It is also possible to have a probe-based framework (such as .NET CLR, which provides hooks to get more information) to generate monitoring data. So, effective instrumentation points themselves can be embedded into the application to facilitate this kind of monitoring. On top of it, the underlying infrastructure, where microservices are hosted, can also raise critical events. These events can be listened to and recorded by the monitoring agents present on the same host as that of the application.

- **Real user monitoring:** This strategy is based on a real end user's transactional flow across the system. While the end user is using the system in real time, the parameters related to the response time and latency, as well as the number of errors experienced by the user, can be captured using it. This is useful for specific troubleshooting and issue resolution. With this strategy, the system's hotspot and bottlenecks around service interactions can be captured as well. It is possible to record the entire end-to-end user flow or transactions to replay it at a later time. The benefits of this are that these kinds of recorded plays can be used for troubleshooting of issues as well as for various types of testing purposes.

- **Semantic monitoring and synthetic transactions:** The semantic monitoring strategy focuses on business transactions; however, it is implemented through the use of synthetic transactions. In semantic monitoring, as the name suggests, we try to emulate end user flows. However, this is done in a controlled fashion and with dummy data so you can differentiate the output of the flow from the actual end user flow data. This strategy is typically used for service dependency, health checking, and diagnostics of problems occurring across the system. To implement synthetic transactions, we need to be careful while planning the flow; also, we need to be careful enough not to stress the system out. Here's an example: creating fake orders for fake product catalogs and observing the response time and output across this whole transaction propagating in the system.

- **Profiling:** This approach is specifically focused on solving performance bottlenecks across the system. This approach is different from the preceding approaches. Real and semantic monitoring focuses on business transactions or functional aspects of the system and collects data around it. Rather, profiling is all about system-level or low-level information capture. A few of these parameters are response time, memory, or threads. This approach uses a probing technique in the application code or framework and collects data. Utilizing the data points captured during the profiling, the relevant DevOps team can identify the cause of the performance problem. Profiling using probing should be avoided on production environments. However, it is perfectly fine to generate call times and so on without overloading the system at runtime. A good example of profiling, in general, is an ASP.NET MVC application profiled with an ASP.NET miniprofiler or even with Glimpse.

- **Endpoint monitoring:** With this approach, we expose one or more endpoints of a service to emit diagnostic information related to the service itself as well as the infrastructure parameters. Generally, different endpoints focus on providing different information. For example, one endpoint can give the health status of the service, while the other could provide the HTTP 500 error information that occurred in that service execution. This is a very helpful technique for microservices since it inherently changes the monitoring from being a push model to a pull model and reduces the overhead of service monitoring. We can scrap data from these endpoints at a certain time interval and build a dashboard and collect data for operational metrics.

Logging

Logging is a type of instrumentation made available by the system, its various components, or the infrastructure layer. In this section, we will first visit logging challenges and then discuss strategies to reach a solution for these challenges.

Logging challenges

We will first try to understand the problem with log management in microservices:

- To log the information related to a system event and parameter as well as the infrastructure state, we will need to persist log files. In traditional .NET monoliths, log files are kept on the same machine where the application is deployed. In the case of microservices, they are hosted either on virtual machines or containers. But virtual machines and containers are both ephemeral, which means they do not persist states. In this situation, if we persist log files with virtual machines or containers, we will lose them. This is one of the challenges of log management in microservices.
- In the microservice architecture, there are a number of services that constitute a transaction. Let's assume we have an order placement transaction where service A, service B, and Service C take part in the transaction. If, say, service B fails during the transaction, how are we going to understand and capture this failure in logs. Not only that but more importantly, how are we going to understand that a specific instance of service B has failed and it was taking part in the said transaction? This scenario presents another challenge in microservices.

Logging strategies

To implement logging in microservices, we can use the key logging strategies discussed next.

Centralized logging

There is a difference between centralized logging and centralized monitoring. In centralized logging, we log all the details about the events that occur in our system--they may be errors or warnings or just for informational purposes. Whereas in centralized monitoring, we monitor critical parameters, that is, specific information.

With logs, we can understand what has actually happened in the system or a specific transaction. We will have all the details about the specific transaction, such as why it started, who triggered it, what kind of data or resources it recorded, and so on. In a complex distributed system, such as microservices, this is really the key piece of information with which we can solve the entire puzzle of information flow or errors. We also need to treat timeouts, exceptions, and errors as events that we need to log.

The information we record regarding a specific event should also be structured, and this structure should be consistent across our system. So, for example, our structured log entry might contain level-based information to state whether the log entry is for information or an error or whether it's debug information or statistics that's been recorded as a log entry event. The structured log entry must also have a date and time so we know when the event happened. We should also include the hostname within our structured log so that we know where exactly the log entry came from. We should also include the service name and the service instance so we know exactly which microservice made the log entry.

Finally, we should also include a message in our structured logging format, which is the key information associated with the event. So, for example, for an error, this might be the call stack or details regarding the exception. The key thing is that we keep our structured logging format consistent. A consistent format will allow us to query the logging information. Then we can basically search for specific patterns and issues using our centralized logging tool. Another key aspect of centralized logging within a microservice architecture is to make distributed transactions more traceable.

Use of a correlation ID in logging

A correlation ID is a unique ID that is assigned to every transaction. So, when a transaction becomes distributed across multiple services, we can follow that transaction across different services using the logging information. The correlation ID is basically passed from service to service. All services that process that specific transaction receive the correlation ID and pass it to the next service and so on so that they can log any events associated with that transaction to our centralized logs. This helps us hugely when we have to visualize and understand what has happened with this transaction across different microservices.

Semantic logging

Event Tracing for Windows (**ETW**) is a structural logging mechanism where you can store a structured payload with the log entry. This information is generated by event listeners and may include typed metadata about the event. This is nothing but an example of semantic logging. Semantic logging strives for passing additional data along with the log entry so that the processing system can get the context structured around the event. Hence, semantic logging is also referred to as structured logging or typed logging.

As an example, an event that indicates an order was placed can generate a log entry that contains the number of items as an integer value, the total value as a decimal number, the customer identifier as a long value, and the city for delivery as a string value. An order monitoring system can read the payload and easily extract the individual values. ETW is the standard shipped feature with Windows.

In Azure Cloud, it is possible to get your log data source from ETW. The Semantic Logging Application Block developed by Microsoft's patterns and practices team is an example of a framework that makes comprehensive logging easier. When you write events to the custom event source, the Semantic Logging Application Block detects this and allows you to write the event to other logging destinations, such as a disk file, database, e-mail message, and more. You can use the Semantic Logging Application Block in Azure applications that are written in .NET and run in Azure websites, cloud services, and virtual machines.

Monitoring in Azure Cloud

Definitely, there is not even one right-off-the-shelf solution or offering found as of now on Azure or for that matter any cloud provider to the monitoring challenges presented by microservices. Interestingly enough, there are not too many open source tools available that can work with .NET-based microservices.

We are utilizing Microsoft Azure Cloud and cloud services for building our microservices, so it is useful to look for the monitoring capability it comes along with. If you are looking to manage around a couple of hundred microservices, you can utilize a custom monitoring solution (mostly interweaving Powershell scripts) based on a Microsoft Azure-based solution.

We will be primarily focusing on the following logging and monitoring solutions:

- Microsoft Azure Diagnostics: This helps in collecting and analyzing resources through resource and activity logs.
- Application Insights: This helps in collecting all of the telemetry data about our microservices and analyzing them. This is a framework-based approach for monitoring.
- Log Analytics: Log Analytics analyzes and displays data and provides scalable querying capability over collected logs.

Let's look at these solutions from a different perspective. This perspective will help us visualize our Azure-based microservice monitoring solution. A microservice is composed of the following:

1. Infrastructure layer, a virtual machine or an application container (for example, Docker container).
2. Application stack layer, which constitutes the operating system, .NET CLR, and the microservice application code.

Each of these layer components can be monitored as follows:

- Virtual machine: Using Azure Diagnostics Logs
- Docker containers: Using container logs and Application Insights or a third-party container monitoring solution, such as cAdvisor, Prometheus, or Sensu
- Windows operating system: Using Azure Diagnostics Logs and Activity Logs
- A microservice application: Using Application Insights
- Data visualization and metric monitoring: Using Log Analytics or third-party solutions, such as Splunk or ELK stack

Various Azure services come with an activity ID in their log entries. This activity ID is a unique GUID assigned for each request, which can be utilized as a correlation ID during log analysis.

Microsoft Azure Diagnostics

Azure diagnostics logs give us the capability to collect diagnostic data for a deployed microservice. We can also use a diagnostic extension to collect data from various sources. Azure diagnostics is supported by web and worker roles, Azure virtual machines, and all Azure App services. Other Azure services have their own separate diagnostics.

Enabling Azure diagnostics logs and exploring various settings in the Azure app service is easy and available as a toggle switch, as shown in the following screenshot:

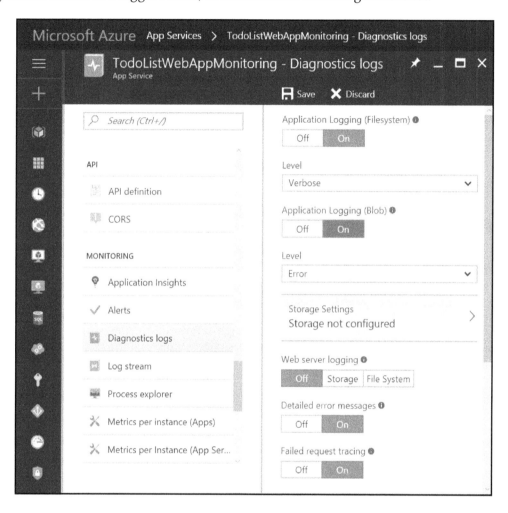

Azure diagnostics can collect data from the following sources:

- Performance counters
- Application logs
- Windows event logs
- .NET event source
- IIS logs
- Manifest-based ETW
- Crash dumps
- Custom error logs
- Azure diagnostic infrastructure logs

Storing diagnostic data using Azure storage

Azure diagnostics logs are not permanently stored. They are rollover logs, that is, they are overwritten by newer ones. So, if we have to use them for any analysis work, we have to store them. Azure diagnostics logs can be either stored in a file system or transferred via FTP; better still, it can be stored in an Azure storage container.

There are different ways to specify an Azure storage container for diagnostics data for the specified Azure resource (in our case, microservices hosted on the Azure app service). These are as follows:

- CLI tools
- PowerShell
- Azure Resource Manager
- Visual Studio 2013 with Azure SDK 2.5 and higher
- Azure portal

Using Azure portal

The following screenshot depicts the Azure storage container provisioned through the Azure portal:

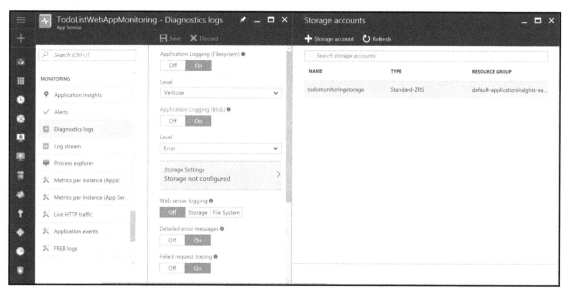

Specifying a storage account

Another way to specify the storage account for storing application-specific diagnostic data is by specifying the storage account in the `ServiceConfiguration.cscfg` file. This is also convenient as during the development time itself, you can specify the storage account. It is also possible to specify an altogether different storage account during development and production. The Azure storage account might also be configured as one of the dynamic environment variables during the deployment process.

The account information is defined as a connection string in a configuration setting. The following example shows the default connection string created for a new microservice project in Visual Studio:

```
<ConfigurationSettings>
<Setting name="Microsoft.WindowsAzure.Plugins.Diagnostics.ConnectionString"
value="UseDevelopmentStorage=true" />
</ConfigurationSettings>
```

You can change this connection string to provide account information for an Azure storage account.

Now, let's see how Azure storage stores the diagnostic data. All the log entries are stored in either a blob or table storage container. The storage choice of can be specified while we create and associate the Azure storage container.

Azure storage schema for diagnostic data

The structure of Azure table storage for storing diagnostic data is as follows:

If the storage is in the form of tables, we will see following tables schema:

- **WadLogsTable:** This table stores the log statements written during code execution, using the trace listener.
- **WADDiagnosticInfrastructureLogsTable:** This table specifies the diagnostic monitor and configuration changes.
- **WADDirectoriesTable:** This table includes the directories that the diagnostic monitor is monitoring. This includes IIS logs, IIS-failed request logs, and custom directories. The location of the blob log file is specified in the container field and the name of the blob is in the RelativePath field. The AbsolutePath field indicates the location and the name of the file as it existed on the Azure virtual machine.
- **WADPerformanceCountersTable:** This table contains data related to the configured performance counters.
- **WADWindowsEventLogsTable:** This table contains Windows' event tracing log entries.

For a blob storage container, the diagnostic storage schema is as follows:

- **wad-control-container:** This is only for SDK 2.4 and previous versions. It contains the XML configuration files that control Azure diagnostics.
- **wad-iis-failedreqlogfiles:** This contains information from the IIS-failed request logs.
- **wad-iis-logfiles:** This contains information about IIS logs.
- **custom:** This is a custom container based on the configuring directories that are monitored by the diagnostic monitor. The name of this blob container will be specified in WADDirectoriesTable.

An interesting fact to note here is that the WAD suffix, which can be seen on these container tables or blobs, comes from Microsoft Azure Diagnostics's previous product name, which is Windows Azure Diagnostics.

> You can use *Cloud Explorer* from Visual Studio to explore the stored Azure diagnostics data.

Introduction of Application Insights

Application Insights is an **application performance management** (**APM**) offering from Microsoft. It is a useful service offering to monitor the performance of .NET-based microservices. It is useful to understand the internal operational behavior of individual microservices. Instead of just focusing on detecting and diagnosing issues, it will tune the service performance and understand the performance characteristic of your microservice. It is one of the examples of a framework-based approach to monitoring. What it means is that during the development of a microservice, we will add the Application Insights package to the Visual Studio solution of our microservice. This is how Application Insights instruments your microservice for telemetry data. This might not always be an ideal approach for every microservice; however, it comes in handy if you have not given any good, thorough thought about monitoring your microservices. This way, monitoring comes out of the box with your service.

With the help of Application Insights, you can collect and analyze the following types of telemetry data types:

- HTTP request rates, response times, and success rates
- Dependency (HTTP & SQL) call rates, response times, and success rates
- Exception traces from both server and client
- Diagnostic log traces
- Page view counts, user and session counts, browser load times, and exceptions
- AJAX call rates, response times, and success rates
- Server performance counters
- Custom client and server telemetry
- Segmentation by client location, browser version, OS version, server instance, custom dimensions, and more
- Availability tests

Along with the preceding types, there are associated diagnostic and analytics tools available for alerting and monitoring with various different customizable metrics. With its own query language and customizable dashboards, Application Insights forms a good monitoring solution for .NET microservices.

Other microservice monitoring solutions

Now let's look at some of the popular monitoring solutions that can be used to build a custom microservice monitoring solution. It is inherent that these solutions do not come out of the box; however, they are definitely time tested by the open source community and can be easily integrated within .NET-based environments.

A brief overview of the ELK stack

As we saw, one of the fundamental tools for monitoring is logging. For microservices, there will be a volume of logs generated that are astounding and sometimes not even comprehended by humans. The ELK stack (also referred to as the elastic stack) is the most popular log management platform. It is also a good candidate for microservice monitoring because of its ability to aggregate, analyze, visualize, and monitor. The ELK stack is a toolchain that includes three distinct tools, namely Elasticsearch, Logstash, and Kibana. Let's visit them one by one to understand their role in the ELK stack.

Elasticsearch

Elasticsearch is full text search engine based on the Apache Lucene library. The project is open source and developed in Java. Elasticsearch supports horizontal scaling and multitenancy and clustered approaches. The fundamental element of Elasticsearch is its search index. This index is stored in forms of JSON internally. A single Elasticsearch server stores multiple indexes (each index represents a database), and a single query can search data with multiple indexes.

Elasticsearch can really provide near real-time searches and can scale with very low latency. The search and results programming model is exposed through the Elasticsearch API and available over HTTP.

Logstash

Logstash plays the role of a log aggregator in the ELK stack. It is a log aggregation engine that collects, parses, processes, and persists the log entries in its persistent store. Logstash is extensive due to its data-pipeline-based architecture pattern. It is deployed as an agent, and it sends the output to Elasticsearch.

Kibana

Kibana is an open source data visualization solution. It is designed to work with Elasticsearch. You use Kibana to search, view, and interact with the data stored in the Elasticsearch indices.

It is a browser-based web application that lets you perform advanced data analysis and visualize your data in a variety of charts, tables, and maps. Moreover, it is a zero configuration application. Therefore, it neither needs any coding nor additional infrastructure after the installation.

Splunk

Splunk is one of the best commercial log management solutions. It can handle even terabytes of log data very easily. Over the period of its existence, it has added many additional capabilities and is now recognized as a full-fledged leading platform for operational intelligence. Splunk is used to monitor numerous applications and environments. It plays a vital role in monitoring any infrastructure and application in real time and is essential to identify issues, problems, and attacks before they impact customers, services, and profitability. Splunk's monitoring abilities, specific patterns, trends and thresholds, and so on can be established as events for Splunk to keep an alert for. This is so that specific individuals don't have to do this manually.

Splunk has an alerting capability included in its platform. So it can trigger alert notifications in real time so that appropriate action can be taken to avoid application or infrastructure downtime.

Based on a trigger of alert and action configured, Splunk can:

- Send an e-mail
- Execute a script or trigger a runbook
- Create an organizational support or action ticket

Typically, Splunk monitoring marks might include the following:

- Application logs
- Active Directory changes events data
- Windows event logs
- Windows performance logs
- WMI-based data
- Windows registry information
- Data from specific files and directories
- Performance monitoring data
- Scripted input to get data from the APIs and other remote data interfaces and message queues

Alerting

Like with any monitoring solution, Splunk also has alert functionalities. It can be configured to set an alert based on any real-time or historical search patterns. These alert queries can be run periodically and automatically, and alerts can be triggered on the results of these real-time or historical queries.

You can base your Splunk alerts on a wide range of threshold- and trend-based situations, such as conditions, critical server or application errors, or threshold amounts of resource utilizations.

Reporting

Splunk can report on alerts that have been triggered and executed as well as if they meet certain conditions. Splunk's alert manager can be used to create a report based on the preceding alert data.

Summary

Debugging and monitoring of microservices is not a simple but a challenging problem. We have used the word *challenging* on purpose: there is no silver bullet for this. There is no single tool that you can install that works like magic. However, with Azure Diagnostics and Application Insights or with ELK stack or Splunk, you can come up with solutions that will help you solve microservice monitoring challenges. Implementing microservice monitoring strategies, such as application/system monitoring, real user monitoring, synthetic transactions, centralized logging, semantic logging block, and implementation of correlation ID throughout transactional HTTP requests, is a helpful way to monitor microservice implementations.

In the next chapter, we will see how we can scale microservices and the solutions and strategies around scaling microservice solutions.

8
Scaling

Imagine you are part of a development and support team that is responsible for developing the company's flagship product: TaxCloud. TaxCloud helps taxpayers file their own taxes and charges them a small fee upon the successful filing of taxes. Consider you had developed this application using microservices. Now say the product gets popular and gains traction, and suddenly, on the last day of tax filing, you get a rush of consumers wanting to use your product and file their taxes. However, the payments service of your system is slow, which has almost brought the system down, and all the new customers are moving to your competitor's product. This is a lost opportunity for your business.

Even though this is a fictitious scenario, it can very well happen to any business. In e-commerce, we have always experienced these kinds of things in real life, especially on special occasions such as Christmas and Black Fridays. All in all, they point toward one major significant characteristic: scalability of the system. Scalability is one of the important non-functional requirements of any mission critical system. Serving to a couple of users having hundreds of transactions is not the same as serving to millions of users having several millions of transactions. In this chapter, we will discuss scalability in general. We'll also discuss how to scale microservices individually and the considerations when we design them and how to avoid cascading failures using different patterns. By the end of this chapter, you will have learned about:

- Horizontal scaling
- Vertical scaling
- The Scale Cube model of scalability
- How to scale infrastructure using Azure scale sets and Docker Swarm
- How to scale a service design through data model caching and response caching
- The Circuit Breaker pattern
- Service discovery

Scalability overview

Design decisions go a long way in impacting the scalability of a single microservice. As with other application capabilities, decisions that are made during the design and early coding phases largely influence the scalability of services.

Microservice scalability requires a balanced approach between services and their supporting infrastructures. Services and their infrastructures also need to scale in harmony.

Scalability is one of the important non-functional characteristics of a system by which it can handle more payload. It is often felt that scalability is usually a concern for large-scale distributed systems. Performance and scalability are two different characteristics of a system. Performance deals with the throughput of the system, whereas scalability deals with serving the desired throughput for a larger number of users or a larger number of transactions.

Scaling infrastructure

Microservices are modern applications and usually take advantage of the cloud. Therefore, when it comes to scalability, the cloud provides certain advantages. However, it is also about automation and managing costs. So even in the cloud, we need to understand how to provision infrastructure, such as virtual machines or containers, to successfully serve our microservice-based application even in the case of sudden traffic spikes.

Now we will visit each component of our infrastructure and see how we can scale it. The initial scaling up and scaling out methods are applied more toward hardware scaling. With the Auto Scaling feature, you will understand Azure virtual manager scale sets. Finally, you will learn about scaling with containers with Docker Swarm mode.

Vertical scaling (scaling up)

Scaling up is a term used for achieving scalability by adding more resources to the same machine. It includes the addition of more memory or processors with higher speed or simply the migration of applications to a more powerful mac

With upgrades in hardware, there is a limit to which you can scale the machine. It is more likely that you are just shifting the bottleneck rather than solving the real problem of improving scalability. If you add more processors to the machine, you might shift the bottleneck to memory. Processing power does not increase the performance of your system linearly. At a certain point, the performance of a system stabilizes even if you add more processing capacity. Another aspect to scaling up is that since only one machine is serving all the requests, it becomes a single point of failure as well.

In summary, scaling vertically is easy since it involves no code changes; however, it is quite an expensive technique. Stack Overflow is one of those rare examples of a .NET-based system that is scaled vertically.

Horizontal scaling (scaling out)

If you do not want to scale vertically, you can always scale your system horizontally. Often, it is also referred to as scaling out. Google has really made this approach quite popular. The Google search engine is running out of inexpensive hardware boxes. So, despite being a distributed system, scaling out helped Google in its early days expand its search in a short amount of time while being inexpensive. Most of the time, common tasks are assigned to worker machines and their output is collected by several machines doing the same task. This kind of arrangement also survives through failures. To scale out, load balancing techniques are useful. In this arrangement, a load balancer is usually added in front of all the clusters of the nodes. So, from a consumer perspective, it does not matter which machine/box you are hitting. This makes it easy to add capacity by adding more servers. Adding servers to clusters improves scalability linearly.

Scaling out is a successful strategy when the application code does not depend upon which server it is running. If the request needs to be executed on a specific server, that is, if the application code has server affinity, it will be difficult to scale out. However, in the case of stateless code, it is easier to get that code executed on any server. Hence, scalability is improved when stateless code is run on horizontally scaled machines or clusters.

Due to this nature of horizontal scaling, it is a commonly used approach across the industry. You can see many examples of large scalable systems managed this way, for example, Google, Amazon, and Microsoft. We recommend that you scale microservices in a horizontal fashion as well.

Microservices scalability

In this section, we will view the scaling strategies available for microservices. We will visit the Scale Cube model of scalability, see how to scale the infrastructure layer for microservices, and embed scalability into the microservice design.

Scale Cube model of scalability

One way to look into scalability is by understanding Scale Cube. In the book *The Art of Scalability: Scalable Web Architecture, Processes, and Organizations for the Modern Enterprise*, *Martin L. Abbott and Michael T.* Fisher defines Scale Cube to view and understand system scalability. Scale Cube applies to microservice architectures as well:

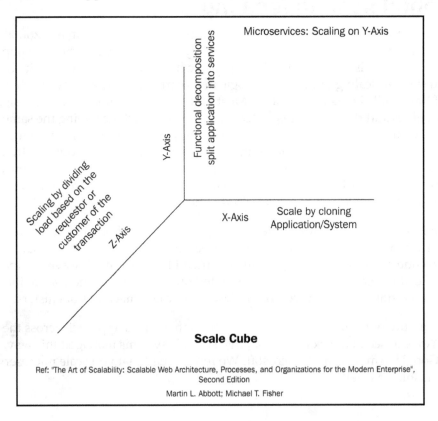

In this three-dimensional model of scalability, the origin (0,0,0) represents the least scalable system. It assumes that the system is a monolith deployed on a single server instance. As shown, a system can be scaled by putting the right amount of effort in three dimensions. To move a system toward the right scalable direction, we need to do the right trade-offs. These trade-offs will help you gain the highest scalability for your system. This will help your system cater to increasing customer demand. This is signified by the **Scale Cube** model. Let's look into every axis of this model and discuss what it signifies in terms of microservices' scalability.

X-axis scaling

Scaling over the *x*-axis means running multiple instances of an application behind a load balancer. This is a very common approach used in monolithic applications. One of the drawbacks of this approach is that any instance of an application can utilize all the data available for the application. It also fails to address application complexity.

Microservices should not share a global state or a kind of data store that can be accessed by all the services. This will create a bottleneck and a single point of failure. Hence, approaching microservices' scaling merely over the *x*-axis of Scale Cube would not be the right approach.

Now let's visit *z*-axis scaling. We have skipped *y*-axis scaling for a reason.

Z-axis scaling

Z-axis scaling is based on a split, which is based on mostly the customer or requestor of a transaction. While *z*-axis splits may or may not address the monolithic nature of instructions, processes, or code, they very often do address the monolithic nature of the data necessary to perform these instructions, processes, or code. Naturally, in *z*-axis scaling, to apply the bias factor, there is one dedicated component responsible. To give an example of a bias factor, it might be a country, request origin, customer segment, or any form of subscription plan associated with the requestor or request. Note that *z*-axis scaling has many benefits, such as improved isolation and caching for requests; however, it also suffers from the following drawbacks:

- It has increased application complexity.
- It needs a partitioning scheme, which can be tricky especially if we ever need to repartition data.
- It doesn't solve the problems of increasing development and application complexity. To solve these problems, we need to apply *y*-axis scaling.

Due to the preceding nature of z-axis scaling, it is not suitable for use in the case of microservices.

Y-axis scaling

Y-axis scaling is based on a functional decomposition of an application into different components. The *y*-axis of Scale Cube represents the separation of responsibility by role or type of data or work performed by a certain component in a transaction. To split the responsibility, we need to split the components of the system as per their actions or role performed. These roles might be based on large portions of a transaction or a very small one. Based on the size of the role, we can scale these components. This splitting scheme is referred to as a *service or resource-oriented splits*.

This very much resembles what we see in microservices. We split the entire application based on their roles or actions, and we scale individual microservice as per its role in the system. This resemblance is not accidental; it is the product of the design. So we can fairly say that *y*-axis scaling is quite suitable for microservices.

Understanding *y*-axis scaling is very significant for scaling a microservice-architecture-based system. So, effectively, we are saying microservices can be scaled by splitting them as per their roles and actions. Consider an order management system that is designed to, say, meet certain initial customer demands; for this, splitting the application into services such as Customer Service, Order service, and Payment service will work fine. However, if demand increases, you would need to review the existing system closely. You might discover the sub components of an already existing service, which can be very well separated again since they are performing a very specific role in that service and the application as a whole. This revisit to design with respect to increased demand/load may trigger resplitting of Order service into Quote service, Order processing service, Order fulfillment service, and so on. Now, definitely, quote service might need more compute power, so we might push more instances (identical copies behind it) as compared to other services.

This is a near real-world example of how we should scale microservices on the AFK Scale Cube's three-dimensional model. You can observe this kind of three-dimensional scalability and *y*-axis scaling of services in some well-known microservice architectures that belong to the industry, such as Amazon, Netflix, and Spotify.

Characteristics of a scalable microservice

In Scale Cube section, we largely focused on scaling the characteristics of an entire system or application. In this section, we will focus on scaling the characteristics of an individual microservice. A microservice is said to be scalable and performant when it exhibits the following characteristics:

- **Known growth curve:** For example, in the case of an order management system, we need to know how many orders are supported by the current services and how they are proportionate to the order fulfillment service metric (measured in "requests per seconds"). The current measured metrics around these are called baseline figures.

- **Well-studied usage metrics:** The traffic pattern generally reveals customer demand and based on customer demand, many parameters mentioned in the previous sections on microservices can be calculated. Hence, microservices are instrumented, and monitoring tools are the necessary companions of microservices.

- **Effective use of infrastructure resources:** Based on qualitative and quantitative parameters, the anticipation of resource utilization can be done. This will help the team predict the cost of infrastructure and plan for it.

- **Ability to measure, monitor, and increase the capacity using an automated infrastructure:** Based on the operational and growth pattern of resource consumption of microservices, it is very easy to plan for future capacity. Nowadays, with cloud elasticity, it is even more important to be able to plan and automate capacity. Essentially, cloud-based architectures are cost-driven architectures.

- **Known bottlenecks:** Resource requirements are the specific resources (compute, memory, storage, and I/O) that each microservice needs. Identifying these are essential for a smoother operational and scalable service. If we identify resource bottlenecks, they can be worked upon and eliminated.

- **Has dependency scaling in the same ratio:** This is self-explanatory. However, you cannot just focus on a microservice, leaving its dependencies as bottlenecks. So microservice is as scalable as its least scaling dependency.

- **Fault tolerant and highly available:** Failures are inevitable in distributed systems. In case you encounter a microservice instance failure, it should be automatically rerouted to a healthy instance of microservice. Just putting load balancers in front of microservice clusters won't be sufficient in this case. Service discovery tools are quite helpful to satisfy this characteristic of scalable microservices.

- **Have scalable data persistence mechanism:** Individual data store choices and design should be scalable and fault-tolerant for scalable microservices. Caching and separating out read and write storage will help in this case.

Now while we are discussing microservices and scalability, the natural arrangement of scaling comes into the picture, which is nothing but the following:

- **Scaling the infrastructure**: Microservices operate well over dynamic and software-defined infrastructures. So, scaling the infrastructure is an essential component of scaling microservices.
- **Scaling around service design**: Microservices' design comprises an HTTP-based API as well as a data store in which the local state for the services is stored.

Scaling the infrastructure

In this section, we will visit all the layers of the microservice infrastructure and see them in relation to each other, that is, how each individual infrastructure layer can be scaled. For our microservice implementation, there are two major components. One is virtual machines and the other is the container hosted on virtual or physical machines. The following diagram shows a logical view of the microservice infrastructure:

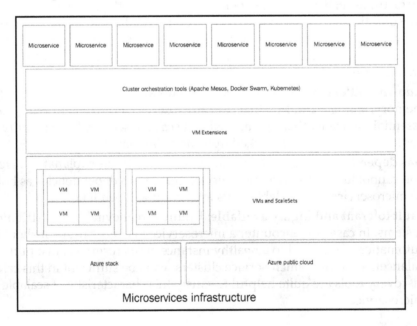

Scaling virtual machines using scale sets

Scaling virtual machines is quite simple and easy in Azure Cloud. This is where microservices shine through. With scale sets, you can raise the instances of the same virtual machine images in a short amount of time, and that automatically too, based on the ruleset. Scale sets are integrated with Azure autoscale.

Azure virtual machines can be created in a way that as a group, they would always serve the requests even if the volume of the requests increases. In specific situations, they can also be deleted automatically, if those virtual machines are not needed to perform the workload. This is taken care of by the virtual machine scale set.

Scale sets also integrate well with load balancers in Azure. Since they are represented as one of the compute resources, they can be used with Azure's resource manager. Scale sets can be configured such that virtual machines can be created or deleted on demand. This helps manage virtual machines with the mindset of `pets vs. cattle`, which we saw in the chapter for deployment.

For applications that need to scale compute resources in and out, scale operations are implicitly balanced across fault and update domains.

With scale sets, you don't need to correlate loops of independent resources, such as NICs, storage accounts, and virtual machines. Even while scaling out, how are we going to take care of the availability of these virtual managers? All such concerns and challenges have already been addressed with virtual machine scale sets.

A scale set allows you to automatically grow and shrink an application based on demand. Let's say there's a threshold of 40 percent utilization. So, maybe once we reach 40 percent utilization, we'll begin to experience performance degradation. And as 40 percent utilization, new web servers gets added. A scale set allows you to set a rule just as mentioned in the previous sections. An input to scale set is a virtual machine. The rules on a scale set says 'at 40 percent average CPU for 5 minutes, Azure will add another virtual machine to the scale set. After doing this, calibrate the rule again. If the performance is still above 40 percent, add a third virtual machine until it reaches the acceptable threshold. Once the performance drops below 40 percent, it will start deleting these virtual machines based on traffic inactivity and so on to reduce your cost of operation.

So by implementing a scale set, you can construct a rule for the performance and make your application bigger to handle greater load by simply automatically adding and removing virtual machines. You, as the administrator, will be left with nothing to do once these rules are established.

Azure autoscale measures performance and determines when to scale up and down. It is also integrated with the load balancer and with NAT. Now the reason they're integrated with the load balancer and with NAT is because as we add these additional virtual machines, we're going to have a load balancer and a NAT device in front. As requests keep coming in, in addition to deploying the virtual machine, we've now got add a rule as well that would allow traffic to be redirected to the new instances. The great thing about scale sets is that they not only add virtual machines but also work with all the other components of the infrastructure, including things such as network load balancers.

In the Azure portal, a scale set can be viewed as a single entry, even though it has multiple virtual machines included in it. To look at the configurations and specification details of virtual machines in a scale set, you will have to use the Azure Resource Explorer tool. It's a web-based tool available at `https://resources.azure.com`. Here you can view all the objects under your subscription. You can view scale sets under the Microsoft.Compute section.

Building a scale set is very easy through the Azure templates repository. Once you create your own **Azure Resource Manager** (**ARM**) template, you can also create custom templates based on scale sets. Due to the scope and space constraints, we have omitted a detailed discussion and instructions on how to build a scale set. You can follow these instructions by utilizing ARM templates given at `https://github.com/gbowerman/azure-myriad`.

 Availability set is an older technology, and this feature has limited support. Microsoft recommends that you migrate to virtual machine scale sets for faster and more reliable autoscale support.

Auto Scaling

With the help of monitoring solutions, we can measure the performance parameters of an infrastructure. This is usually in the form of performance SLAs. Auto Scaling gives us the ability to increase or decrease the resources available to the system, based on performance thresholds.

The Auto Scaling feature adds additional resources to cater to increased load. It goes in the reverse way as well. If load gets reduced, then Auto Scaling reduces the number of resources available to perform the task. Auto Scaling does it all without pre-provisioning the resources and that too in an automated way.

Auto Scaling can scale in both ways: vertically (adding more resources to the existing resource type) or horizontally (adding resources by creating another instance of that type of resource).

The Auto Scaling feature makes the decision of adding or removing resources based on two strategies. One is based on the available metrics of the resource or on meeting some system threshold value. The other type of strategy is based on time, for example, between 9.00 a.m. and 5:00 p.m. IST, instead of three web servers, the system needs 30 web servers.

Azure monitoring instruments every resource; through this, all the metric-related data is collected and monitored. Based on the data collected, auto scaling takes decisions.

Azure Monitor autoscale applies only to virtual machine scale sets, cloud services, and app services--web apps.

Container scaling using Docker swarm

Earlier, in the chapter on deployment, we saw how to package a microservice into a Docker container. We also discussed in detail why containerization is useful in the microservice world. In this section, we will advance our skills with Docker and also see how easily we can scale our microservices with Docker swarm.

Inherently, microservices are distributed systems and need to be distributed and isolated resources. Docker swarm provides container orchestration clustering capabilities so that multiple docker engines can work as a single virtual engine. It is similar to the load balancer capabilities; besides, it also creates new instances of containers or deletes containers, if the need arises.

You can use any of the available service discovery mechanisms, such as DNS, consul, or zookeeper tools, with Docker swarm.

A swarm is a cluster of Docker engines or nodes where you can deploy your microservices as "services." Now, do not confuse these services with microservices. Services is a different concept in Docker implementation. A **service** is the definition of the tasks to execute on the worker nodes. You may want to understand the node we are referring to in the last sentence. The node, in a Docker swarm context, is used for the Docker engine participating in a cluster. A complete swarm demo is possible, and ASP.NET Core images are available at ASP.NET-Docker project on GitHub (`https://github.com/aspnet/aspnet-docker`).

 Azure Container Service has been recently made available. It is a good solution for scaling and orchestrating Linux or Windows containers using DC/OS, Docker swarm, or Google Kubernetes.

Now that we have understood how to scale a microservice infrastructure, let's visit the scalability aspects around the microservice design in our next section.

Scaling service design

In this section, we will visit the components/concerns that need to be taken care of while designing or implementing a microservice. With infrastructure scaling taking care of service design, we can truly unleash the power of the microservice architecture and get a lot of business value around making microservices a true success story. So what are those components in service design; let's have a look.

Data persistence model design

In traditional applications, we have always relied on relational databases to persist user data. Relational databases are not new to us. They emerged in the seventies as the way to store persistent information in a structured way that would allow you to make queries and perform data maintenance.

In today's world of microservices, modern applications need to be scaled at the hyperscale stage. We are not recommending here that you abandon the usage of relational databases in any sense. They still have their valid use cases. However, when we mix read and write operations in a single database, complications arise when we need to have increased scalability. Relational databases enforce relationships and ensure consistency of data. Relational databases work on the well-known ACID model. So, in relational databases, we use the same data model for both read and write operations.

However, the needs of read and write operations are quite different. In most cases, read operations usually have to be quicker than write operations. Read operations can also be done using different filter criteria, returning a single row or a result set. In most write operations, there is a single row or column involved, and usually, write operations take a bit longer duration of time as compared to read operations. So either we can optimize and serve reads or optimize and serve writes in the same data model.

How about we split the fundamental data model into two halves: one for all the read operations and the other for all the write operations? Now things become far simpler, and it is easy to optimize both the data models with different strategies. The impact of it on our microservices is that they, in turn, become highly scalable for both kinds of operations.

This particular architecture is known as Common Query Responsibility Segregation (CQRS). As a natural consequence, CQRS also gets extended in terms of our programming model. Now the database-object relationship between our programming models has become much simpler and scalable.

With this comes our next fundamental element in scaling a microservice implementation: caching of data.

Caching mechanism

Caching is the simplest way to increase the application's throughput. The principle is very easy. Once the data is read from data storage, it is kept as close as possible to the processing server. In future requests, the data is served directly from the data storage or cache. The essence of caching is minimizing the amount of work that a server has to do. HTTP has a built-in cache mechanism embedded in the protocol itself. This is the reason it scales so well.

With respect to microservices, we can cache at three levels, namely client side, proxy, and at server side. Let's look at each of them.

First we have client-side caching. With client side caching, clients store cached results. So the client is responsible for doing the cache invalidation. Usually, the server provides guidance, using mechanisms such as cache-control and expiry headers, about how far it can keep the data and when it can request fresh data. With browsers supporting HTML5 standards, there are more mechanisms available, such as local storage, an application cache, or a Web SQL database, in which the client can store more data.

Next, we move onto the proxy side. Many reverse proxy solutions, such as squid, HAProxy, and Nginx, can act as cache servers as well.

Now let's discuss server-side caching in detail. In server-side caching, we have the following two types:

1. Response caching: This is an important kind of caching mechanism for a web application UI, and honestly, it is simple and easy to implement as well. In response caching, cache-related headers get added to the responses served from microservices. It can drastically improve the performance of your microservice. In ASP.NET Core, you can implement response caching using the `Microsoft.AspNetCore.ResponseCaching` package.

2. Distributed caching for persisted data: A distributed cache enhances microservice throughput due to the fact that cache will not cost an I/O trip to any external resource. This has the following advantages:
   - Microservice clients get the exact same results.
   - Distributed cache is backed up by a persistence store and runs as different remote processes. So even if the app server restarts or has any problem, it in no way affects the cache.
   - The source's data store has fewer requests made to it.

You can use distributed providers, such as Redis or memcache, in clustered mode for scaling your microservice implementation.

Redundancy and fault tolerance

We understand that a system's ability to deal with failures and recover from those failures are not the same as that offered by scalability. However, we cannot also deny that they are closely related abilities of the system. Unless we address the concerns of availability and fault tolerance, it will be challenging to build highly scalable systems. In a general sense, we achieve availability through making redundant copies available to different parts/components of the system. So, in this section, we will shortly touch base upon two such concepts.

Circuit breakers

A circuit breaker is a safety feature in an electronic device that, in the event of a short circuit, breaks the electricity flow and protects the device or prevents any further damage to the surroundings. This exact idea can be applied to software design. When a dependent service is not available or not in a healthy state, a circuit breaker prevents calls from going to that dependent service and redirects the flow to an alternate path for a configured period of time.

In his famous book, *Release It! Design and Deploy Production-Ready Software*, Michael T. Nygard gives details about the circuit breaker. A typical circuit breaker pattern is shown in the following diagram:

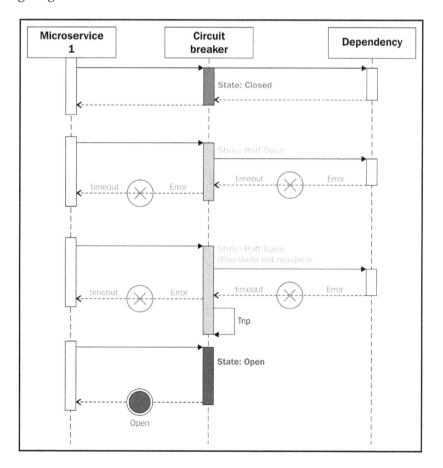

As shown in the diagram, the circuit breaker acts as a state machine with three states.

Closed state

This is the initial state of the circuit, which depicts a normal flow of control. In this state, there is a failure counter. If OperationFailedException occurs in this flow, the failure counter is increased by one. If the failure counter keeps increasing, meaning the circuit encounters more exception, and reaches the failure threshold set, the circuit breaker transitions to an **Open** State. But if the calls succeed without any exception or failure, the failure count is reset.

Open state

In the **Open** state, a circuit has already tripped and a timeout counter has started. If a timeout is reached and a circuit still keeps on failing, the flow of code enters into the **Half-Open** state.

Half-Open state

In the **Half-Open** state, the state machine/circuit breaker component resets the timeout counter and again tries to open the circuit, reinitiating the state change to **Open** state. However, before doing so, it tries to perform regular operations, say, a call to the dependency; if it succeeds, then instead of the **Open** state, the circuit breaker component changes the state to **Closed**. This is so that the normal flow of operation can happen and the circuit is closed again.

For .NET-based microservices, if you want to implement the circuit breaker and a couple of fault-tolerant patterns, there is a good library named *Polly* available in the form of a NuGet package. It comes with extensive documentation and code samples, and moreover, has a fluent interface. You can add Polly from `http://www.thepollyproject.org/` or by just issuing the install--Package Polly command from the package manager console in Visual Studio.

Service discovery

For a small implementation, how can you determine the address of a microservice? For any .NET developer, the answer is that we simply put the IP address and port of service in the configuration file and we are good. However, when you deal with hundreds or thousands of them dynamically configured at runtime, we understand we have a service location problem.

Now if you peek a bit deeper, we are trying to solve two parts of the problem:

1. **Service registration**: This is nothing but the process of registration within the central registry of some kind where all the service-level metadata, hosts' list, ports, and secrets are stored.
2. **Service discovery**: Establishing communication at runtime with a dependency through a centralized registry component is nothing but service discovery.

Any service registration and discovery solution needs to have the following characteristics to make it considerable as a solution for the microservice services discovery problem and they are:

- The centralized registry itself should be highly available
- Once a specific microservice is up, it should receive the requests automatically
- Intelligent and dynamic load balancing capabilities should exist in the solution
- The solution should be able to monitor the capability over service health status and the load it is subjected to
- The service discovery mechanism should be capable of diverting the traffic to other nodes or services from unhealthy nodes without any downtime or without any impact on its consumers
- If there is a change in the service location or metadata, the service discovery solution should be able to apply the changes without impacting the existing traffic or service instances

Some of the service discovery mechanisms are available within the open source community. They are as follows:

- **Zookeeper**: Zookeeper (`http://zookeeper.apache.org/`) is a centralized service for maintaining configuration information, naming, providing distributed synchronization, and providing group services. It's written in Java, is strongly consistent (CP), and uses the Zab (`http://www.stanford.edu/class/cs347/reading/zab.pdf`) protocol to coordinate changes across the ensemble (cluster).
- **Consul**: Consul makes it simple for services to register themselves and discover other services via a DNS or HTTP interface. It registers external services, such as SaaS providers, as well. It also acts as a centralized configuration store in the form of key values. It also has failure detection properties. It is based on the peer-to-peer gossip protocol.

- **Etcd:** Etcd is a highly available key-value store for shared configuration and service discovery. It was inspired by Zookeeper and Doozer. It's written in go,and uses Raft (`https://ramcloud.stanford.edu/wiki/download/attachments/11370504/raft.pdf`) for consensus, and has an HTTP- plus JSON-based API.

Summary

Scalability is one of the critical advantages of pursuing the microservice architectural style. We saw the characteristics of microservice scalability. We discussed the Scale Cube model of scalability and how microservices can scale on the y-axis by functional decomposition of the system. Then we approached the scaling problem with the scaling infrastructure. In the infrastructure segment, we saw strong capability of Azure Cloud to scale, utilizing the Azure scale sets and container orchestration solutions, such as Docker swarm, DC/OS, and kubernates.

In later stages of the chapter, we focused on scaling with a service design and discussed how our data model should be designed; we also discussed considerations, such as having a split CQRS style model, while designing the data model for high scalability. We also briefly touched on caching, especially distributed caching, and how it improves the throughput of the system. In the last section, to make our microservices highly scalable, we discussed the circuit breaker pattern and service discovery mechanism, which are essential for the scalability of our microservice architecture.

In the next chapter, we will see the reactive nature of microservices and the characteristics of reactive microservices.

9
Reactive Microservices

We have now gained a clear understanding of a microservice-based architecture and how to harness its power. Until now, we've discussed various aspects of this architecture, such as communication, deployment, and security, in detail. We also saw how microservices collaborate among themselves when required. Now let's take the effectiveness of microservices to the next level by introducing the reactive programming aspect within them. We will cover the following topics:

- Understanding reactive microservices
- Mapping processes
- Communication in reactive microservices
- Handling security
- Managing data
- The microservice ecosystem

What are reactive microservices?

Before we dive into reactive microservices, let's see what the word *reactive* means. There are certain fundamental attributes that a piece of software must possess in order to be considered reactive. These attributes are responsiveness, resilience, elasticity, and above all, being message-driven. We'll discuss these attributes in detail and see how they can make microservices a stronger candidate for most enterprise requirements.

Responsiveness

It wasn't long ago when one of the key requirements of business sponsors, discussed in requirement gathering sessions, was a guaranteed response time of a few seconds. For example, a t-shirt custom print e-shop where you could upload images and then have it rendered on the chosen piece of apparel. Move forward a few years and I can vouch for this myself; I will close the browser window if any web page takes longer than a couple of seconds to load.

Users today expect near instantaneous response. But this is not possible unless the code that you write follows certain standards to deliver the expected performance. There would always be so many different components cooperating and coordinating together to solve some business problem. The time that each component is expected to return the results in has therefore reduced to milliseconds today. Also, the system has to exhibit consistency along with performance when it comes to response time. If you have a service that exhibits variable response times over a defined period, then it is a sign of an impending problem in your system. You will have to sooner or later deal with this baggage. And there is no doubt that in most cases, you will manage to solve it.

However, the challenge is much bigger than what is visible from the surface. Any such trait needs to be probed for a possibility of an issue in the design. It could be some kind of dependency on another service, too many functions performing at the same time within the service, or synchronous communication blocking the workflow at some point.

Resilience

With all the buzz around distributed computing, what does a user expect from such a system in the event of a failure of one or more components? Does a single failure result in a catastrophic domino effect resulting in the failure of the entire system? Or, does the system bounce back from such an event with grace and within expected timelines? The end user shouldn't be affected at all in such scenarios, or the system should at least minimize the impact to an extent ensuring that user experience is not affected.

Reactive microservices take the concept of microservices to the next level. As the number of microservices grows, so does the need for communication across them. It won't be very long before the task of tracking a list of a dozen other services, orchestrating a cascading transaction between them, or just the requirement of generating a notification across a set of services becomes a challenge. For the scope of this chapter, the concept of cascading is more important than the transaction itself. Instead of the transaction, it could very well be just the need of notifying some external system based upon some filtering criteria.

The challenge arises as an enterprise-level microservice-based system would always extend far beyond a handful of microservices. The sheer size and complexity of this cannot be pictured fully here in a chapter. In such a scenario, the need to track a set of microservices and communicate with them can quickly become a nightmarish scenario.

What if we could take away the responsibility of communicating an event to other microservices from individual microservices? The other aspect of this could very well be freedom for the services from tracking others in the ecosystem for a possible trigger. To do this, you will have to keep track of their whereabouts. Just add authentication to this and you could very easily be tangled in the mess you never signed up for.

The solution lies in a design change where the responsibility of tracking microservices for an event or communicating an event to others is taken away from individual microservices.

While transitioning from a monolithic application to a microservice-styled architecture, we saw how they are isolated. Through seam identification, we isolated modules into independent sets of services that own their data and don't allow other microservices/processes to access them directly. We achieved autonomy by catering to a single business functionality and taking care of aspects such as its data and encapsulated business functionality. Asynchronous was another characteristic that we achieved for our microservices in order to make non-blocking calls to it.

Autonomous

All along, we have been strongly advocating the correct isolation of microservices. Seam identification was a concept we briefly touched upon in `Chapter 2`, *Building Microservices*. There were numerous benefits that we derived while successfully implementing the microservice-styled architecture. We can safely state that isolation is one of the fundamental requirements here. However, the benefits of successful implementation of isolation go much beyond it.

It is very important for microservices to be autonomous, else our work will be incomplete. Even after implementing the microservice architecture, if one microservice failure results in delay for other services or a domino effect, it means we missed something in our design. However, if microservice isolation is done right along with the right breakdown of the functionality to be performed by this particular microservice, it would mean that the rest of the design would fall into place itself to handle any kind of resolution conflict, communication, or coordination.

The information required to perform such an orchestration would depend primarily on the well-defined behavior of the service itself. So the consumer of a microservice that is well-defined doesn't need to worry about the microservice failing or throwing an exception. In case there is no response within the stipulated period of time, just try again.

Being message-driven

Being message-driven is the core of reactive microservices. All reactive microservices define, as part of their behavior, any event that they might be generating. These events may or may not have additional information payload with them, depending upon the design of the individual event. The microservice that is the generator of this event would not be bothered about whether the event generated was acted upon or not. Within the scope of this specific service, there is no behavioral definition for the action beyond the generation of this event. For it, the scope ends there. It is now for the rest of the system comprising other microservices to act upon this information, based upon their individual scope.

The difference here is that all these events being generated could be captured asynchronously by listening to them. No other service is waiting in blocking mode for any of these services. Anyone listening to these events is called a subscriber, and the action of listening for the events is called subscribing. The services that subscribe to these events are called observers, and the source service of the events generated is termed **Observable**. This pattern is termed the **Observer Design Pattern**.

However, the very exercise of having a concrete implementation on each of the observers is somewhat inconsistent with our motto of designing loosely coupled microservices. If this is what you are thinking, then you have the right thinking cap on and we are on the right track. In a short while from now, while mapping our processes as reactive microservices, we will see how we can achieve this purpose in the world of reactive microservices.

Before we go on with mapping our processes, it is important that we briefly discuss the pattern with respect to our topic here. In order to act upon a message, you first need to show your intent to watch the message of that type. At the same time, it is required that the originator of the message has an intent to publish such a message to the interested observers. So there would be at least one observable to be observed by one or more observers. To add some spice to it, the observable can publish more than one type of message, and the observers can observe one or more of the messages they intend to act upon.

The pattern doesn't restrict observers from unsubscribing when they want to stop listening for these messages. So it sounds pretty, but is it as easily implemented? Let's move ahead and see this for ourselves.

Making it reactive

Let's examine our application and see how it would look with the reactive style of programming. The following image depicts the flow of the application that is reactive in nature and is completely event-driven. In this image, services are depicted by hexagons, and events are represented by square boxes. Here's the entire flow in detail:

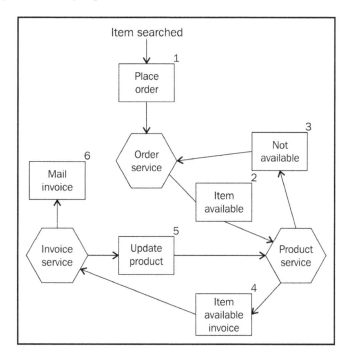

The flow depicted in the image describes the scenario of a customer placing an order after having searched for the items he/she is looking for. The **Place order** event is raised to **Order service**. In response to this event, our service analyzes arguments, such as order item and quantity, and raises the **Item availability** event to **Product service**. From here on, there are two possible outcomes: either the requested product is available and has the required quantity or it is not available or doesn't have the required quantity. If the items are available, **Product service** raises an event called **Generate invoice** to **Invoice service**. Since raising the invoice means confirming the order, the items in the invoice would no longer be available in stock; we need to take care of this and update the stock accordingly. To handle this, our invoice service further raises an event called **Update Product Quantity** to **Product service** and takes care of this requirement. For the sake of simplicity, we will not go into the details of who will handle the event of **Mail Invoice**.

Event communication

The preceding discussion may have left you thinking about how the event being raised maps the call of the respective microservice perfectly; let's discuss this in further detail. Think of all the events being raised as being stored in an event store. The event stored has an associated delegate function that is called to cater to the respective event. Although it is shown that the store has just two columns, it stores much more information, such as details of the publisher, subscriber, and so on. Each event contains the complete information that is required to trigger the corresponding service. So event delegation might be a service to be called or a function within the application itself. It doesn't matter to this architecture.

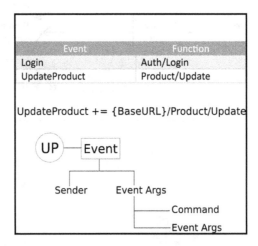

Security

There are numerous ways in which security can be handled while implementing reactive microservices. However, given the limited time and scope that we have here, we will restrict our discussion to one type only. Let's go on and discuss message-level security here and see how it is done.

Message-level security

Message-level security is the most fundamental way available to secure your individual request messages. After the initial authentication is performed, the request message itself could contain the OAuth bearer token or the JWTs, based on the implementation. This way, each and every request is authenticated, and the information related to the user could be embedded within these tokens. The information could be as simple as a username along with an expiration timestamp indicating token validity. After all, we don't want to allow a token to be utilized beyond a certain extent of time.

However, it is important to note here that you are free to implement it in such a manner that a lot more information could be embedded and utilized for different uses.

Scalability

There is another aspect you need to consider here as well. Within this token, we could also embed authorization information apart from authentication information. Although, note that having all of this information within a token that is being passed around frequently could soon become an overhead. We can make the necessary changes to ensure that the information pertaining to the authorization is a one-time activity and is later persisted with the services as required.

When we decide to persist authorization-related information with individual services, we make them elastic in a way. The task of persisting authorization information with individual services will do away with the requirement of reaching out to the authentication service each time for authorization-related data. This means we can scale our services quite easily.

Communication resilience

What would happen if the authentication service that contains all the user authentication data and authorization data become unavailable? Does this mean that the entire microservice ecosystem would come down to its knees, as all the actions or a big percentage of them would need to be authorized for the user attempting the action? This does not fit the domain of the microservice architecture. Let's see how we could deal with this.

One way could be to replicate user authorization data within each service that requires it. When the authorization data is already available with the respective services, it will reduce the data being transferred through the JWTs being moved around. What this would achieve is that in the event our Auth service becomes unavailable, the users who are authenticated and have accessed the system would not be affected. With all of the authorization data already available within the individual services that need to verify it, the business can continue as usual without any hindrances.

However, this approach comes with a price of its own. It will become a challenge to maintain this data as it is updated all the time with all the services. The replication required for each service would be an exercise in itself. There is a way out of this specific challenge as well, though.

Instead of making this data available in all the microservices, we could simply store it in a central store and have the services validate/access authorization-related data from this central store. This would enable us to build resilience beyond the authentication service.

Managing data

Tracking a single order being placed is easy. However, multiply that number with the million orders being placed and canceled every hour; it could quickly become a challenge in the reactive microservices domain. The challenge is how you would perform a transaction across multiple services. Not only is it difficult to track such a transaction, it poses other challenges, such as persisting such a transaction that spans the database and message broker. The task of reversing such an operation in the likelihood of the transaction breaking somewhere in the middle due to a service failure could be even more daunting.

In such a scenario, we can utilize the event sourcing pattern. This is a strong candidate, especially since we are not looking for a two-phase commit, generally referred to as 2PC. Instead of storing a transaction, we persist all the state-changing events of our entities. In other words, we store all the events that change their states in the form of entities, such as order and product. When a client places an order, then under regular circumstances, we would persist the order to the order table as a row. However, here we will persist the entire sequence of events, reaching up to the final stage of the order being accepted or rejected.

Refer to the preceding image where we analyzed the sequence of events that are generated while creating an order. See how those events will be stored in this pattern and how a transaction would be deduced from that set of events. First, let's see how the data will be stored. As seen in the following image, individual records are saved as rows. Data consistency is confirmed post the transaction.

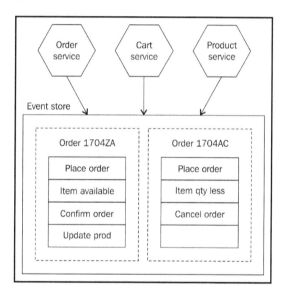

As seen in the following image, the **Product service** can subscribe to the order events and update itself accordingly. There are numerous benefits to be derived from this approach, such as:

- Since the events are being persisted, the challenge of recognizing a transaction is separated from the task of maintaining database integrity
- It is possible to find the exact state of the system at any given point in time

- It is easier to migrate a monolith with this approach
- It is possible to move back in time to a specific set of events and identify any possible problems

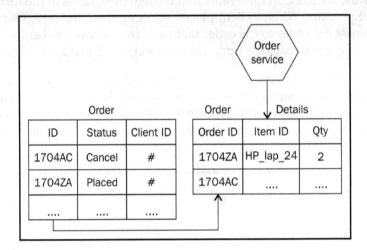

Apart from all the benefits, it has some drawbacks as well. The most important one is how to query the event store. To reconstruct the state of a given business entity at a given point in time would require some level of complex queries. Apart from this, there would be a learning curve involved to grasp the concept of an event store replacing the database and then deducing the state for an entity. Query complexity can be handled with the help of the CQRS pattern easily. However, this will be outside the scope of this chapter. It will be worthwhile to note that the event sourcing pattern and CQRS deserve separate chapters in the wake of reactive microservices.

The microservice ecosystem

As discussed in the initial chapters, we need to get ready for big changes when embracing microservices. The discussions we've had on deployment, security, and testing so far would have had you thinking by now about accepting this fact. Unlike monoliths, adoption of microservices requires you to prepare beforehand and in a way that you start building the infrastructure along with it and not after it. In a way, microservices thrive in the complete ecosystem where everything is worked out, from deployment to testing and security to monitoring. The returns associated with embracing such a change are huge. There is definitely a cost involved to make all these changes. However, instead of having a product that doesn't get on the market, it is better to incur some costs and design and develop something that thrives and does not die out after the first few rollouts.

Reactive microservices - coding it down

Now, let's try to sum up everything and see how it actually looks in the code. We will use Visual Studio 2015 for this. The first step would be to create a reactive microservice, then we will move on to creating a client for consuming the service created by us.

Creating the project

We will now go ahead and create our reactive microservice example. In order to do this, we need to create a project of the ASP.NET web application type. Just follow these steps and you should be able to see your first reactive microservice in action:

1. Start Visual Studio.
2. Create a new project by navigating to **File** | **New** | **Project**.
3. From the installed templates, select **Web** and **ASP.NET Web Application**.
4. Name it `FlixOne.BookStore.ProductService.Tests` and click on **OK**.
5. Next, select **Empty** from the template screen and check the **WebAPI** option for adding folders and core references. Then click on **OK**:

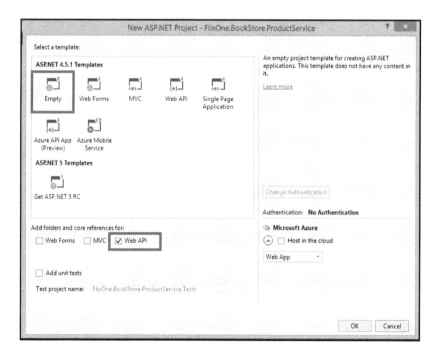

6. Add folders' persistence and context to the project:
7. Add the following NuGet packages to the project:
   - Reactive.Core.
   - EntityFramework.

8. Add the Product.cs model to the Models folder:

```
using System;

namespace FlixOne.BookStore.ProductService.Models
{
    public class Product
    {
        public Guid Id { get; set; }
        public string Name { get; set; }
        public string Description { get; set; }
        public string Image { get; set; }
        public decimal Price { get; set; }
        public Guid CategoryId { get; set; }

        public virtual Category Category { get; set; }
    }
}
```

9. Add the Category.cs model to the Models folder:

```
using System;
using System.Collections.Generic;

namespace FlixOne.BookStore.ProductService.Models
{
    public class Category
    {
        public Category()
        {
            Products = new List<Product>();
        }

        public Guid Id { get; set; }
        public string Name { get; set; }
        public string Description { get; set; }
        public IEnumerable<Product> Products { get; set; }
    }
}
```

We have created our models. Our next step would be to add the code for interacting with the database. These models help us project data from a data source into our models.

Let's create a context, namely `ProductContext`, while deriving it from `DbContext`. In one of the preceding steps, we created a folder named `Context`. Add the `ProductContext.cs` file to it. The class named `ProductContext` would house our context. The Entity Framework context helps query the database. Also, it helps us collate all the changes that we perform on our data and execute them on the database in one go. The following is the code for `DbContext`. We will not go into detail about Entity Framework or the contexts because they are not part of the scope here:

```
using System.Data.Entity;
using FlixOne.BookStore.ProductService.Models;

namespace FlixOne.BookStore.ProductService.Contexts
{
    public class ProductContext : DbContext
    {
        public ProductContext()
            : base("name=ProductDBConnectionString")
        {
        }
        public DbSet<Product> Products { get; set; }

        public DbSet<Category> Categories { get; set; }
    }
}
```

This context would pick the connection string from the `web.config` file in the `connectionString` section--a key named `ProductDBConnectionString`. You could name it anything, but remember to use the same name in the constructor of the context, shown in the preceding class:

```
<connectionStrings>
<add name="ProductDBConnectionString" connectionString="Data
Source=KANWARS\SQLEXPRESS;Initial Catalog=ProductDB;Integrated
Security=true"
providerName="System.Data.SqlClient"/>
</connectionStrings>
```

With our context in place and taking care of the communication between our application and the database, let's go ahead and add a repository for facilitating interaction between our data models and our database. The following is the code for our repository:

```
using System;
using System.Collections.Generic;
using System.Data.Entity;
using System.Linq;
using System.Reactive;
```

```
using System.Reactive.Concurrency;
using System.Reactive.Linq;
using FlixOne.BookStore.ProductService.Contexts;
using FlixOne.BookStore.ProductService.Models;

namespace FlixOne.BookStore.ProductService.Persistence
{
    public class ProductRepository : IProductRepository
    {
        private readonly ProductContext _context;

        public ProductRepository(ProductContext context)
        {
            _context = context;
        }

        public IObservable<IEnumerable<Product>> GetAll()
        {
            return Observable.Return(GetProducts());
        }

        public IObservable<IEnumerable<Product>> GetAll(IScheduler
            scheduler)
        {
            return Observable.Return(GetProducts(), scheduler);
        }

        public IObservable<Unit> Remove(Guid productId)
        {
            return Remove(productId, null);
        }

        public IObservable<Unit> Remove(Guid productId, IScheduler
        scheduler)
        {
            DeleteProduct(productId);

            return scheduler != null
                ? Observable.Return(new Unit(), scheduler)
                : Observable.Return(new Unit());
        }

        private IEnumerable<Product> GetProducts()
        {
            var products = (from p in
            _context.Products.Include("Category")
                orderby p.Name
                select p).ToList();
```

```
            return products;
        }

        private Product GetBy(Guid id)
        {
            return GetProducts().FirstOrDefault(x => x.Id == id);
        }

        private void DeleteProduct(Guid productId)
        {
            var product = GetBy(productId);
            _context.Entry(product).State = EntityState.Deleted;
            _context.SaveChanges();
        }
    }
}
```

Marking our result from `GetAll` as `IObservable` adds that reactive functionality we are looking for. Also, pay special attention to the return statement.

With this observable model, it becomes possible for us to handle streams of asynchronous events with the same ease we are used to while handling other simpler collections:

```
return Observable.Return(GetProducts());
```

We are now ready to expose the functionality through our controllers. Add a file named `ProductController` while deriving the class from `ApiController` to the `Controllers` folder. Here is what our controller would look like:

```
using System;
using System.Collections.Generic;
using System.Reactive.Linq;
using System.Threading.Tasks;
using System.Web.Http;
using FlixOne.BookStore.ProductService.Contexts;
using FlixOne.BookStore.ProductService.Models;
using FlixOne.BookStore.ProductService.Persistence;

namespace FlixOne.BookStore.ProductService.Controllers
{
    public class ProductController : ApiController
    {
        private readonly IProductRepository _productRepository;

        public ProductController()
        {
            _productRepository = new ProductRepository(new
            ProductContext());
```

```
            }
            public ProductController(IProductRepository
    productRepository)
            {
                _productRepository = productRepository;
            }
            [HttpGet]
            public async Task<IEnumerable<Product>> Get()
            {
                var observable = _productRepository.GetAll();
                var arrayResult = observable.SelectMany(p =>
    p).ToArray();

                return await arrayResult;
            }
        }
    }
```

The final structure looks similar to the following image in the Solution Explorer:

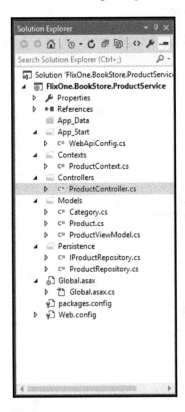

To create the database, you can refer to the *EF Core migrations* section in `Chapter 2`, *Building Microservices*, or simply call the Get API of our newly deployed service. When the service finds out that the database doesn't exist, the entity framework code's first approach in this case will be to ensure that the database is created.

We can now go ahead and deploy this service for our client. With our reactive microservice deployed, we now need a client to call it.

Client - coding it down

We will create a web client for consuming our newly deployed reactive microservice with the help of AutoRest. Let's create a console application for it and add Nuget packages: `Reactive.Core, WebApi.Client, Microsoft.Rest.ClientRuntime`and `Newtonsoft.Json`.

1. AutoRest would add a folder named `Models` to the main project and create copies of the model's product and category, as in the service that we just created. It will have necessary deserialization support built into in.
2. ProductOperations.cs and ProductServiceClient.cs contain the main plumbing required for all the calling.
3. In the `Main` function of the `Program.cs` file, change the `Main` function as follows:

```
static void Main(string[] args)
{
    var client = new ProductServiceClient {BaseUri =
    new Uri("http://localhost:22651/")};
    var products = client.Product.Get();
    Console.WriteLine($"Total count {products.Count}");
    foreach (var product in products)
    {
        Console.WriteLine($"ProductId:{product.Id},Name:
        {product.Name}");
    }
    Console.Write("Press any key to continue ....");
    Console.ReadLine();
}
```

At this point, if the database is not created, then it will be created as required by the Entity Framework.

We need to know how is this list, which is returned from our microservice, different from the regular list. The answer is that if this were a non-reactive scenario and you were to make any changes in the list, it would not be reflected on the server. In the case of reactive microservices, changes that are made to such a list would be persisted to the server without having to go through the process of tracking and updating the change manually.

You would have noticed that we had to do very little or no work at all when it came to messy callbacks. This helps keep our code clean and easier to maintain. With observable, it is the producer that pushes the values when they are available. Also, there is a difference here that the client is not aware of: whether your implementation is blocking or non-blocking. To the client, it all seems like asynchronous.

You are left alone to focus more on important tasks than to figure out what call to be made next or which one you missed altogether.

Summary

In this chapter, we added the aspect of reactive programming to our microservice-based architecture. There are trade-offs with this message-driven approach to microservices communicating with each other. However, at the same time, this approach tends to solve some of the fundamental problems when we advance our microservice architecture further. The event sourcing pattern comes to our rescue and lets us get past the limitation of an ACID transaction or a two-phase commit option. This topic requires a separate book altogether and restricting it to a single chapter does not do justice to it. We used our sample application to understand how to restructure our initial microservice in a reactive way.

In the next chapter, we would have the entire application ready for us to explore and we will put together everything that we have discussed so far in this book.

10
Creating a Complete Microservice Solution

On our journey down the lane of understanding microservices and their evolution, we continued through various phases. We explored what led to the advent of microservices and the various advantages of utilizing them. We also discussed various integration techniques and testing strategies. Let's recap all that we have talked about thus far:

- Testing microservices
- Security
- Monitoring
- Scaling
- Reactive microservices

Architectures before microservices

Microservices were never designed from the ground up to be in the present form. Instead, there has been a gradual transition from other forms of prevalent architecture styles to microservices. Prior to microservices, we had the monolithic architecture and service-oriented architecture that reigned over the world of enterprise development.

Let's delve into these two before doing a quick recap of microservices and their various attributes and advantages.

The monolithic architecture

The monolithic architecture has been around for quite some time and it results in self-contained software with a single .NET assembly. It consists of the following components:

- User interface
- Business logic
- Database access

The cost paid for being self-contained was that all the components were interconnected and interdependent. A minor change in any module had the capability to impact the entire piece of software. With all the components so tightly coupled in this manner, it made testing the entire application necessary. Also, another repercussion of being so tightly coupled was that the entire application had to be deployed once again. Let's sum up all the challenges we faced as a result of adopting this style of architecture:

- Large interdependent code
- Code complexity
- Scalability
- System deployment
- Adoption of a new technology

Challenges in standardizing the .NET stack

Technology adoption is not easy when it comes to monolithics. It poses certain challenges. Security, response time, throughput rate, and technology adoption are some of them. It is not that this style of architecture does not fight back with solutions. The challenge is that in monolithics, code reusability is really low or absent, which makes any exercise an expensive affair to implement.

Scaling

We also discussed how scaling is a viable option but with diminishing returns and increasing expenses. Both vertical and horizontal scaling have their own pros and cons. Vertical scaling is seemingly easier to begin with: investing in IT infrastructures, such as RAM upgrades and disk drives. However, the return plateaus out very quickly. The disadvantage of the downtime required for vertical scaling doesn't exist in horizontal scaling. However, beyond a point, the cost of horizontal returns becomes too high.

Service-oriented architecture

Another widely used architecture in the industry was a **service-oriented architecture** (**SOA**). This architecture was a move away from the monolithic architecture and was involved in resolving some of its challenges, mentioned in the preceding section. To begin with, it was based on a collection of services. Providing service was the core concept of SOA.

A service is a piece of code, program, or software that provides some functionality to other system components. This piece of code was able to interact directly with the database or indirectly through other services. It was self-contained to the extent that it allowed services to be consumed easily by both desktop or mobile applications.

Some of the definite advantages that SOA provided over monolithic were:

- Reusability
- Stateless
- Scalability
- Contract-based
- Ability to upgrade

Microservice-styled architecture

Apart from some of the definite advantages of SOA, microservices provide certain additional differentiating factors that makes it a clear winner. At the core, microservices were defined to be completely independent of other services in the system and run in their process. The attribute of being independent required certain discipline and strategy in the application design. Some of the benefits it provides are:

- **Clear code boundaries**: This resulted in easier code changes. It has independent modules provided an isolated functionality that led to a change in one microservice has little impact on others.
- **Easy deployment**: It is possible to deploy one microservice at a time if required.
- **Technology adaptation**: The preceding attributes led to the gain of this much sought after benefit. This allows us to adopt different technologies in different modules.
- **Affordable scalability**: This allows us to scale only chosen components/modules instead of the whole application.
- **Distributed system**: This comes implied, but a word of caution is necessary here. Make sure that your asynchronous calls are used well and the synchronous ones don't block the whole flow of information. Use data partitioning well. We will come to this a little later, so don't worry for now.
- **Quick market response**: In a competitive world, this is a definite advantage as users tend to quickly lose interest if you are slow to respond to new feature requests or adopt a new technology within your system.

Messaging in microservices

This is another important area that needs its share of discussion. There are primarily two main types of messaging utilized in microservices:

- Synchronous
- Asynchronous

Monolith transitioning

As part of our exercise, we decided to transition our existing monolithic application FlixOne to a microservice-styled architecture. We saw how to identify decomposition candidates within a monolith, based on the following parameters:

- Code complexity
- Technology adoption
- Resource requirement
- Human dependency

There are definite advantages it provides in regard to cost, security, and scalability apart from technology independence. This also aligns the application more with the business goals rather than the current or possible technical boundaries.

The entire process of transitioning requires you to identify seams that act like boundaries of your microservices along which you can start the separation. You have to be careful about picking up seams on the right parameters. We have talked about how module interdependency, team structure, database, and technology are a few probable candidates. Special care is required to handle master data. It is more a choice whether you want to handle master data through a separate service or through configurations. You will be the best judge based as per your scenario. The fundamental requirement of a microservice having its own database is that you remove many of the existing foreign key relationships. This would bring forth the need to intelligently pick your transaction-handling strategy to preserve data integrity.

Integration techniques

We have already explored synchronous and asynchronous ways of communication between microservices and discussed the collaboration style of the services. These styles were Request/Response and event-based. Though Request/Response seems to be synchronous in nature, the truth is that it is the implementation that decides the outcome of this style of integration. Event-based style, on the other hand, is purely asynchronous.

When dealing with a large number of microservices, it is important that we utilize an integration pattern in order to facilitate complex interaction among microservices. We explored the API Gateway along with an event-driven pattern.

API Gateway provides you with a plethora of services; some of which are as follows:

- Routing an API call
- Verifying API keys, JWT tokens, and certificates
- Enforcing usage quotas and rate limits
- Transforming APIs on the fly without code modifications
- Setting up caching backend responses
- Logging call metadata for analytics purposes

The event-driven pattern works by some services publishing their events and some subscribing to those available events. The subscribing services simply react independently of the event-publishing services, based on the event and its metadata. The publisher is unaware of the business logic that the subscribers would be executing.

Deployment

Monolith deployments for enterprise applications can be challenging for more than one reason. Having a central database, which is difficult to break down, only increases the overall challenge along with time to market.

For microservices, the scenario is much different. The benefits don't just come by virtue of the architecture being microservices. Instead, it is the planning from the initial stages itself. You can't expect an enterprise-scale microservice to be managed without **continuous delivery** (**CD**) and **continuous integration** (**CI**). So strong is the requirement for CI and CD right from the early stages that without it, the production stage may never see the light of the day.

Tools such as CFEngine, chef, puppet, ansible, and powershell DSC help you represent an infrastructure with code and let you easily make different environments exactly the same. Azure could be an ally here. The rapid and repeated provisioning required here could easily be met with it.

Isolation requirement could be met with containers far more effectively than its closest rival, virtual machines. We have already explored Docker as one of the popular candidates for containerization and have seen how to deploy them.

Testing microservices

We all know the importance of unit testing and why every developer should be writing these more often than not. Unit tests are a good means to verify the smallest of the functionality that contributes toward building larger systems.

However, testing microservices is not a routine affair like testing a monolith since one microservice might interact with a number of other microservices. In that case, should we utilize the calls to the actual microservices to ensure that the complete workflow is working fine? The answer is no, as this would make developing a microservice dependent on another piece. If we do this, then the whole purpose of having a microservice-based architecture is lost. In order to get around this, we will use the mock and stub approach. This approach not only makes the testing independent of other microservices, but also makes testing with databases much easier since we can mock database interactions as well.

Testing a small isolated functionality with a unit test or testing a component by mocking the response from an external microservice has its scope and it works well within that scope. However, if you are already asking yourself the question about testing the larger context, then you are not alone. Integration testing and contract testing are the next steps in testing your microservices.

In integration testing, we're concerned about external microservices and communicate with them as part of the process. For this purpose, we mock external services. We take this further with contract testing, where we test each and every service call independently and then verify the response as well. An important concept worth spending time on is consumer-driven contracts. Refer to `Chapter 4`, *Testing Strategies*, for studying this in detail.

Security

The traditional approach of having a single point of authentication and authorization worked well in the monolithic architecture. However, in the case of microservices, you would need to put efforts into doing this for each and every service. This would pose a challenge of not only implementing the same but keeping it synchronized as well.

The OAuth 2.0 authorization framework and OpenID Connect 1.0 specifications combined together can solve the problem for us. OAuth 2.0 describes all the roles involved in the authorization process that suffices our needs pretty well. We just have to make sure that the right kind of grant type is picked up; otherwise, the security will be compromised. OpenID Connect authentication is built on top of the OAuth 2.0 protocol.

Azure Directory (Azure AD) is one of the providers of OAuth 2.0 and OpenID Connect specifications. It is understood here that Azure AD scales very well with applications and integrates well with any organizational Windows Server Active Directory.

As we have already discussed containers, it is important and interesting to understand that containers are very close to the host operating system's kernel. Securing them as well is another aspect that can't be overrated. Docker was the tool we considered, and it provides the necessary security by means of the least privilege principle.

Monitoring

The monolith world had a few advantages of its own. Easier monitoring and logging is one of those areas where things are easier compared to microservices. The sheer number of microservices across which an enterprise system might be spread can be mind-boggling.

As discussed in `Chapter 1`, *What are Microservices*, in the *Prerequisites for a microservice architecture* section, an organization should be prepared for the profound change. The monitoring framework was one of the key requirements for this.

Unlike a monolith architecture, monitoring is very much required from the very beginning in a microservice-based architecture. There is a wide range of reasons why monitoring can be categorized:

- **Health**: We need to preemptively know when a service failure is imminent. Key parameters, such as CPU and memory utilization, along with other metadata could be a precursor to either the impending failure or just a flaw in the service that needs to be fixed. Just imagine an insurance company's rate engine getting overloaded and going out of service or even performing slow when a few hundred field executives try to share the cost with the probable clients. Nobody likes to wait these days.

- **Availability**: There might a situation when the service may not perform extensive calculations, but the bare availability of the service itself might be crucial to the entire system. In such a scenario, I remember relying upon pings to listeners that would wait for a few minutes before shooting out e-mails to the system administrators. It worked for monoliths with one or two services to be monitored. However, with microservices, much more metadata comes into the picture.

- **Performance**: For platforms receiving high footfall, such as banking and e-commerce, availability alone does not deliver the service required. Considering the number of people converging at their platforms in very short spans, ranging from a few minutes to even tens of seconds, performance is not a luxury anymore. You need to know how the system is responding by means of data, such as concurrent users being served, and compare that with the health parameters in the background. This might provide an e-commerce platform with the ability to decide whether upgrades are required before the upcoming holiday season. For more sales, you need to serve a higher number of people.

- **Security**: In any system, you can plan resilience only up to a specific level. No matter how well designed a system is, there would be thresholds beyond which the systems will falter, which can result in a domino effect. However, having a thoughtfully designed security system in place could easily avert DoS and SQL Injection attacks. This would really matter from system to system when dealing with microservices. So think ahead and think carefully when setting up trust levels between your microservices. The default strategy that I have seen people utilizing is securing the endpoints with microservices. However, covering this aspect increases the depth of your system's security and is worthwhile spending some time with.

- **Auditing**: Domains such as healthcare, financing, and banking are a few domains that have the most strict compliance standards around all associated services. And it is pretty much the same world over. Depending upon the kind of compliance you are dealing with, you might have a requirement to keep the data for a specific period of time as a record, keep the data in a specific format to be shared with regulatory authorities, or even sync with systems provided by the authority. Taxation systems could be another example here. With a distributed architecture, you don't want to risk losing the data record set related to even a single transaction since that would amount to compliance failure.

- **Troubleshooting system failures**: This, I bet, would be a favorite for a long time to come to anybody who is getting started with microservices. I remember the initial days when I use to try troubleshooting a scenario involving two Windows services. I never thought of recommending a similar design again. But time has changed and so has the technology today.

When providing a service to other clients, monitoring becomes all the more important. As in today's competitive world, SLA would be part of any deal and has a cost associated with it in the event of both success and failure. Ever wondered how easily we assumed that the Microsoft Azure SLA would stand true come what may? I have myself grown so used to it that the queries from the clients worried about cloud resource availability are answered with a flat reply of 99.9 percent uptime without even a blink of an eye.

So unless you can't be confident of agreeing on an SLA to your clients when providing a service, they can't count on it to promise the same SLA forward. As a matter of fact, no SLA might mean that your services are probably not stable enough to provide one.

Monitoring challenges

There could be multiple key points that need to be addressed before you could have a successful monitoring system in place. These need to be identified and assigned a solution to. Some of the key points are discussed next.

Scale

If you have a successfully running system with a few dozen microservices orchestrating successful transactions in perfect harmony, then you have won the first battle. Congratulations! However, you must plug in the necessary monitoring part if you haven't done so already. Ideally, this should be part of step one itself.

Component lifespan

With the use of virtual machines and containers, we need to figure out what part is worth monitoring. Some of these components would be already nonexistent by the time you look at the data generated by monitoring them. So it becomes extremely important that you choose the information to be monitored wisely.

Information visualization

There are tools available, such as AppDynamics and New Relic, that would allow you to visualize the data for maybe up to 10-100 microservices. However, in real-world applications, this is just a fraction number. There has to be clarity about the purpose of this information and well-designed visualization around it. This is one area where we can opt for reverse design. First, think about the report/visualization you want and then see what and how it is to be monitored.

Monitoring strategies

To begin with monitoring, you could think of different commonly implemented strategies as a solution to your problem. Some of the commonly implemented strategies are:

- Application/system monitoring
- Real user monitoring
- Semantic monitoring and synthetic transactions
- Profiling
- Endpoint monitoring

Just bear in mind that each one of these strategies is focused on solving a specific purpose only. While one could be helpful in analyzing transaction propagation, the other could be suitable for testing purposes. So it is important for you to pick up a combination of these when designing the whole system since just using a single strategy won't suffice the needs.

Scalability

We have discussed in detail the scale-cube model of scalability and have found what scaling at each axis means. Note that x-axis scaling is achieved through the use of load balancers between multiple instances and the users of the microservices. We also saw how z-axis scaling is based on the transaction origination suffered from some drawback.

Broadly, scaling in the microservice world can be categorized under two separate heads:

1. Infrastructure
2. Service design

Infrastructure scaling

Virtual machines are an indispensable component of the microservice world. The features available as part of the Microsoft Azure platform enable you to easily perform this seemingly complex task without breaking a sweat.

Through the scale set feature, which is integrated with Azure autoscale, we can easily manage a set of identical virtual machines.

Auto scaling lets you define thresholds for various supported parameters, such as CPU usage. Once the threshold is breached, the scale set kicks in, based on whether the parameters scale in or scale out.

This means that if the scale set predicts that it needs to add more virtual machines to cater to the increased load, it will continue to do so until the thresholds are back to normal. Similarly, if the demand for resource being governed falls, it will decide to remove the virtual machine from the scale set. To me, this sounds like peace for the networking team. The options around auto scaling can be explored further as it is capable of taking care of complex scaling requirements, running into hundreds of virtual machines while scaling in or scaling out.

Service design

In our microservices, we have already achieved the isolation of data for each microservice. However, the model for reading and writing to the database is still the same. With the underlying relational databases enforcing the ACID model, this can be a costly affair. Or we can say that this approach can be slightly modified to implement the database read and write operation in a different way.

We can employ the common query responsibility segregation, also referred to as CQRS, for making effective design changes in our microservices to handle this. Once the model-level separation is done, we will be free to optimize the read and write data models using a different strategy.

Reactive microservices

We have progressed well while transitioning our monolithic application to the microservice-styled architecture. We have also briefly touched upon the possibility of introducing reactive traits to our services. We now know what are the key attributes of reactive microservices are:

- Responsiveness
- Resilience
- Autonomous
- Being message-driven

We also saw the benefits of reactive microservices amounting to less work on our part when it comes to managing communication across/between the microservices. This benefit translates not just into reduced work but the capability to focus on the core job of executing the business logic instead of trying to grapple with the complexities of inter-service communication.

Greenfield application

Now let's go ahead and create the FlixOne bookstore from scratch. First, we will scope out our microservices and their functionalities and identify inter-service interactions as well.

Our FlixOne bookstore will have the following set of functionalities available:

- Searching through the available books
- Filtering books on the basis of categories
- Adding books to the shopping cart
- Making changes to the shopping cart
- Placing an order from the shopping cart
- User authentication

Scoping our services

In order to understand how these functionalities will map out as different microservices, we need to first understand what it would take to support it and what can be clubbed together as a microservice. We will see how the data store would start to look out of the window of microservices themselves.

The book-listing microservice

Let's try to break down the first functionality of searching through books. In order to let our users browse through the store for books, we need to maintain a list of books on offer first. Here we have our first candidate being carved out as a microservice. The book catalogue service would be responsible for not just searching through the available books, but also maintaining the data store that would house all the information pertaining to books. The microservice should be able to handle various updates required for the available books in the system. We will call it the book catalog microservice. And, it will have its own book data store.

The book-searching microservice

Examining the next functionality of filtering books seems to be coming under the purview of the book catalog microservice itself. However, having said that, let's confirm it by questioning our own understanding of the business domain here. The question that comes to my mind is related to the impact of all the searches that our users would perform, bringing down the service. So should the book search functionality be a different service? Here the answer lies in the fact that the microservice should have its own data store. Having the book catalog and the book catalog search function as different services would require us to maintain a list of books in two different locations with additional challenges, such as having to sync them. The solution is simple: have a single microservice, and if required, scale up and load balance the book catalogue microservice.

The shopping cart microservice

The next candidate is the one made famous by the online shopping revolution brought around by the likes of Amazon and further fuelled by smartphones: the shopping cart microservice. It should let us add or remove books to our cart before we finally decide to check out and pay for them. There is no doubt whether this should be a separate microservice or not. However, this brings forth an interesting question of whether it deals with the product's data store or not; it would need to do this in order to receive some fundamental details, such as availability in stock. Accessing the data store across the service is out of question as that is one of the most fundamental prerequisite for microservices. The answer to our question is inter-service communication. It is OK for a microservice to use the service provided by another microservice. We will call this our shopping cart microservice.

The order microservice

The business functionality of placing an order is next in line. When a user decides that his shopping cart has just the right books as required, he/she decides to place an order. At that moment in time, some information related to the order has to be confirmed/conveyed to various other microservices. For example, before the order is confirmed, we need to confirm from the book catalog that there is enough quantity available in stock to fulfil the order. Post this confirmation, the right number of items are supposed to be reduced from the book catalog. The shopping cart would also have to be emptied post the successful confirmation of the order.

Although our order microservice sounds more pervasive and in contradiction to the rules of non-sharing of data across microservices, it is not the case, as we will see shortly. All the operations will be completed while maintaining clear boundaries, with each microservice managing its own data store.

User authentication

Our last candidate is the user authentication microservice that would validate the user credentials of customers who log into our book store. The sole purpose of this microservice is to confirm whether or not the provided credentials are correct in order to restrict unauthorized access. This seems pretty simple for a microservice; however, we have to remember the fact that making this functionality a part of any other microservice would impact more than one business functionality when you decide to change your authentication mechanism. The change may come in form of using JWT tokens being generated and validated based on the OAuth 2.0 authorization framework and OpenID Connect 1.0 authentication.

The following is the final list of candidates for microservices:

1. The book catalog microservice
2. The shopping cart microservice
3. The order microservice

4. The user authentication microservice

Synchronous versus asynchronous

Before we get started with a brief introduction of microservices, there is an important point to consider here. Our microservices will be communicating with each other, and there is a possibility that they will rely on a response to move further. This poses a dilemma for us, having gone through all the pain of unlearning the beloved monolithic and then getting into the same situation where a point of failure can be a cascading collapse of the system.

The book catalog microservice

This microservice has six main functions exposed through an HTTP API component. It is the responsibility of this HTTP API component to handle all the HTTP requests for these functions. These functions are:

API resource description	API resource description
GET /api/book	Gets a list of the available books
GET /api/book{category}	Gets a list of the books for a category
GET /api/book{name}	Gets a list of the books by name
GET /api/book{isbn}	Gets a book as per the ISBN number
GET /api/bookquantity{id}	Gets the available stock for the intended book
PUT /api/bookquantity{id, changecount}	Increase or decrease the available stock quantity for a book

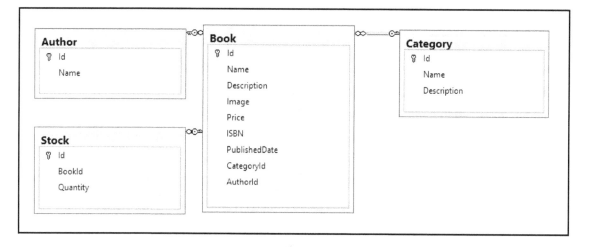

The shopping cart microservice

This microservice will have the following functions exposed as HTTP endpoints for consumption:

API resource description	API resource description
POST /api/book {customerid }	Adds the specific book to the shopping cart of the customer
DELETE /api/book {customerid }	Removes the book from the shopping cart of the customer
GET /api/book{customerid}	Gets the list of books in the shopping cart of the customer
PUT /api/empty	Removes all the books currently contained in the shopping cart.

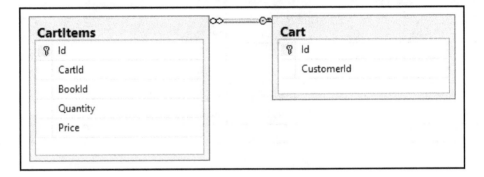

The order microservice

This microservice will have the following functions exposed as HTTP endpoints for consumption.

API resource description	API resource description
POST /api/order {customerid }	Gets all the books in the shopping cart of the customer and creates an order for the same
DELETE /api/order {customerid }	Removes the book from the shopping cart of the customer
GET /api/order{orderid}	Gets all the books as part of the specific order

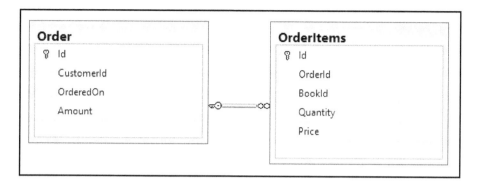

The user auth microservice

This microservice will have the following functions exposed as HTTP endpoints for consumption.

API resource description	API resource description
GET /api/verifyuser{customerid, password}	Verifies the user

You can look at the application source code and analyze it as required.

Summary

We hope that this book was able to get you initiated with the fundamental concepts of the microservice-styled architecture and also helped you dive deeply into the fine aspects of microservices with clear examples to associate the concepts with. The final application is available for you to take a closer look and analyze what you have learned so far at your pace. We wish you luck in utilizing the skills learned in this book and apply them to your real-world challenges.

Index

www.ingramcontent.com/pod-product-compliance
Lightning Source LLC
Chambersburg PA
CBHW060530060326
40690CB00017B/3438